THE
MotoGP
MISCELLANY

I dedicate my book to my editor, Martin Corteel, and to my proofreader, Jo.

Martin, thank you for offering me the chance to write this book,
the 15th Sports Miscellany we have published together.

Jo, without your invaluable help in checking over my work,
this book would never have been published.

John

This edition published 2016

Carlton Books Limited
20 Mortimer Street
London W1T 3JW

A CIP catalogue record for this book is available from the British Library

ISBN: 978-1-78097-763-8

Commissioning Editor: Martin Corteel
Assistant Editor: David Ballheimer
Project Art Editor: Luke Griffin
Production: Maria Petalidou

Printed in Dubai

JOHN WHITE

THE
MOTOGP
MISCELLANY

WITH A FOREWORD BY
JOHN SURTEES CBE

CARLTON
BOOKS

❀ FOREWORD ❀

It was 1940. I was six years old and, with my mother, brother and sister, had been evacuated to be near my father at Catterick. He was helping train despatch riders and organize the workshops. We had been bombed out, but something that travelled with us was a tea chest of magazines. One made a lasting impression; it was *Motorcycling* and featured a picture of Georg Meier standing on the footrests of his BMW Kompressor Grand Prix bike going down Bray Hill to win the Isle of Man TT.

Fast forward to 1950, and I was about to have my first ever road race on the new Brands Hatch circuit. The World Championship scene was largely a contest between Great Britain and Italy, with home teams of Norton, AJS and Velocette competing against Moto Guzzi, Gilera and MV Agusta. The four-cylinder Gilera of Umberto Masetti won the 500cc Championship by one point from Geoff Duke on the Norton.

I was to experience using the same techniques of negotiating Bray Hill in the Isle of Man TT as Georg Meier. It was a different type of racing to the short circuits on which I had previously raced, but something that had to be done if you were to compete in the World Championship and a very different and special challenge in any case.

We have seen many changes over the years. The arrival of the Japanese; they had looked and realized racing's potential to develop their personal skills and technology, and to publicize their fledgling motorcycle industry. It didn't take them long to contest all classes and, in the senior class, only MV Agusta, in the early Seventies, continued to fight. But it was not to last. Fortunately, we still have the Italian challenge with, in particular, European hopes resting on Ducati.

So, to say that Japanese machines have not dominated the world of MotoGP, as it is now called, would be an understatement. What is important, however, is that in seeking to dominate the world of motorcycling, Yamaha, Honda, Kawasaki and Suzuki have given young riders from many nations the opportunity to develop and achieve great things on the track. I am not going to mention any specific names, but over the years we have seen some superb champions.

The machines have changed dramatically and the techniques required to get the utmost performance out of them have also changed. But something I don't think does change is the competitiveness in people who want to express themselves by coming together with a motorcycle in looking to get the ultimate performance from it. The satisfaction that comes from becoming as one with a machine in order to achieve this is something that will always be close to my heart. I am sure that this is what enthrals all those followers of MotoGP at the track and on the screen as they see the riders all trying their utmost to achieve this.

Through this book you can learn more about the history and names that have made headlines over the years and their achievements.

John Surtees CBE

❂ INTRODUCTION ❂

John McGuinness's superb voiceover introduction to the DVD, *TT3D Closer to the Edge*, sums up what it is like to ride a factory-built motorcycle in the Isle of Man TT: "It's the most exhilarating place in the world. It's like being able to fly. Just like growing wings. It's in your blood. You just can't get it out. You just want more."

Formula One motor racing moves the body but MotoGP moves the soul. Memories of Nigel Mansell cocooned in the cockpit of a Ferrari taking the Parabolica, the signature corner at Monza, in the Italian Grand Prix, just does not have the same thrill as watching Giacomo Agostini fly over Bray Hill in the 1968 Isle of Man TT on the famous Snaefell Mountain Course on the island. F1 drivers take the Parabolica at race speeds approaching 150mph and total concentration and bravery is a pre-requisite as the corner lasts for an incredible 7.5 seconds. Bray Hill is one of the most difficult sections of the 37.7-mile (60.3km) circuit which snakes its way round the island. Today riders complete Bray Hill, which finishes with a bump that causes the bikes to leave the road, at speeds approaching 200mph, and this is followed by an immediate steep rise at Quarterbridge which makes bikes "wheelie-up" a stretch of road known as "Ago's Leap" in honour of Agostini.

If Formula 1 oozes glamour and speed, then MotoGP bleeds greater speed, excitement and thrill-a-minute chases. The fastest speed ever recorded for a MotoGP bike is 217.66mph (349.23kmh), set by Marc Marquez on a Honda RC213V at the 2015 German GP. MotoGP, or at least the 500cc World Championship, predates the Formula 1 World Championship by a year, and in the 67 seasons of motorcycle racing's elite class, there have been thrilling duels, exhilarating performances, magnificent machines, flamboyant racers and, tragically, too many losses of the men who brought enjoyment and excitement to millions of motorcycle racing fans around the world.

This book was inspired by the men who have made the sport the spectacle of speed it is today, such as Agostini, Sheene – my own personal hero of the paddock – and seven-times MotoGP World Champion Valentino Rossi, who once said, "The most important thing is to have a good relationship with the bike. You have to understand what she wants. I think of a motorcycle as a woman, and I know that sounds silly, but it's true." Who could argue with Rossi, who almost tied Agostini's eight world titles in the senior class?

Grazie Giacomo e Valentino and Cheers Barry.

John D.T. White
Spring 2016

● 1949 500CC FINAL STANDINGS (TOP 10) ●

Pos	Rider	Nationality	Bike	Pts
1.	Leslie Graham	(GBR)	AJS	30
2.	Nello Pagani	(ITA)	Gilera	29
3.	Arciso	(ITA)	Gilera	25
4.	Bill Doran	(GBR)	AJS	23
5.	Artie Bell	(GBR)	Norton	20
6.	Harold Daniell	(GBR)	Norton	17
7.	Johnny Lockett	(SPA)	Norton	13
8.	Enrico Lorenzetti	(ITA)	Moto Guzzi	7
9.	Ernie Lyons	(IRL)	Velocette	7
10.	Giani Leoni	(ITA)	Moto Guzzi	6

● CONSTRUCTORS' FINAL STANDINGS (TOP 5) ●

Pos	Team	Nationality	Pts
1.	AJS	(GBR)	32
2.	Gilera	(ITA)	31
3.	Norton	(GBR)	25
4.	Moto Guzzi	(ITA)	13
5.	Velocette	(GBR)	12

● FROM FIGHTER PLANES TO MOTORBIKES ●

In 1945, Richard "Dickie" Dale, born 25 April 1927, was drafted into the Royal Air Force as a flight mechanic and during his time at RAF Cranwell he purchased his first bike, a 1939 AJS Silver Streak. He loved racing bikes and, in 1949, racing for AJS, he competed in one round of the inaugural 350cc F.I.M. Motorcycle Road Racing World Championships, finishing sixth in the Ulster GP. In his career, which lasted from 1949–60, he won two Grand Prix races, the 500cc Spanish Grand Prix on an MV Agusta in 1954, and a year later, the 350cc Nations Grand Prix at Monza, this time on a Moto Guzzi. Dale finished fourth in the 500cc World Championship in both 1954 and 1958, and finished second in the 1955 and 1956 350cc World Championship, beaten – in both years – by his Moto Guzzi team-mate, Bill Lomas. On 30 April 1961, he raced in the Eifelrennen Race at the 7.747km (4.814-mile) Sudschleife circuit of the Nurburgring, Germany. Dale won the 350cc race on a Norton, and entered another Norton in the 500cc race. Tragically, he lost control on the very fast Bocksberg Curve, crashed into a roadside post and died in the helicopter taking him to hospital.

❂ THE RACING SHEPHERD ❂

Alan Shepherd's career ran from 1958 to 1964, and he rode in every class from 125cc to 500cc. His most successful seasons were in 1962 and 1963, when riding for Matchless. He finished runner-up behind MV Agusta's Mike Hailwood in both 500cc World Championships. In all, Shepherd won two Grand Prix races, the 1962 500cc Finnish GP for Matchless and the 1964 250cc United States Grand Prix for East German manufacturer MZ. He suffered serious head injuries in a crash while testing late in 1964 and, although he made a full recovery, he elected to retire in 1965 as he did not think he could continue to be a top rider – he was in the top division with Honda – and do justice to the bike. Shepherd died, aged 71, in July 2007.

Did You Know That?
Alan Shepherd had three wins in Northern Ireland's North West 200: the 350cc race in 1960 and the 350cc and 500cc races in 1962.

❂ KEEPING HIS MEMORY ALIVE ❂

Every night as the sun begins to set in Coriano, Italy, a huge flame is ignited and burns in memory of Marco Simoncelli, who died on 23 October 2011 in the Malaysian MotoGP Grand Prix. Coriano was Marco's home town and the flame burns for exactly 58 seconds, in honour of his race number.

❂ PODIUM FIZZ ❂

Freixenet Cordon Negro, the official MotoGP sparkling wine, is described by the producers as a crisp, clean, well-balanced Cava, with a palate of apple, ripe pear and bright citrus flavours, plus a touch of ginger. They believe it is a bubbly that means business – especially when it gets sprayed all over you in the moment of triumph!

❂ DONINGTON PARK CORNERS ❂

Redgate ❖ Hollywood ❖ Craner Curves ❖ Old Hairpin ❖ Starkey's Bridge ❖ Schwantz Curve ❖ McLean's ❖ Coppice ❖ Roberts Chicane ❖ Fogarty Esses ❖ Melbourne Hairpin ❖ Goddards

Did You Know That?
The two main Donington Park straights are Starkey's and Wheatcroft.

● GEOFF DUKE – WATER FLOWING FROM A TAP ●

Geoffrey Ernest Duke was born on 29 March 1923 in St Helens, Lancashire, England. His parents – his father was a baker – did not want him to ride motorcycles after his older brother Eric was knocked off his motorbike and was severely injured. Thankfully for the world of motorcycle racing, his parents relented and Geoff bought a 1923 belt-drive Raleigh, with two friends, for 10 shillings. He got his first job, a telephone engineer with the Post Office, in 1939 and, in 1942, volunteered for military service, joining the Royal Corps of Signals, where Geoff became a riding instructor. After being demobbed, he worked for BSA and then for Norton, where he became a member of the trials team. His riding style, described by Irish motorcyclist Stanley Woods as "water flowing from a tap", made Norton sit up and take note of the talent they had at their disposal.

Geoff made his racing debut in the 1948 Junior Isle of Man TT on a 350cc Norton borrowed from the factory. He performed impressively, leading after three laps, but a split oil tank forced his retirement. The following year, he won his first road race, beating Les Graham (who would become the inaugural 500cc World Champion that year) in the 350cc at Haddenham and then won the Senior Manx Grand Prix as well as the Senior Clubman's TT, both times on a Norton. Towards the end of 1949, Geoff – always looking for anything which would increase his speed over his rivals – came up with a lightweight, close-fitting suit with minimal pockets and padding. He visited a local tailor, Frank Barker, with his sketches. Between them, they designed an aerodynamic leather outfit which weighed less than 5lb (2.275kg). In 1950, Geoff joined the Norton works team and was runner-up in the Isle of Man Junior TT (won by Artie Bell on another Norton) and broke the lap and race records winning the Senior TT. He finished the year as runner-up – by a single point – to 500cc World Champion Umberto Masetti (Gilera), and missed out by six points on the 350cc World Championship, too, beaten only by Bob Foster (Velocette).

Geoff was unstoppable in 1951, becoming World Champion in both the 500cc and 350cc classes for Norton. He retained his 350cc crown in 1952, but left Norton to ride for the Italian factory team, Gilera, in 1953 and reeled off three consecutive 500cc World Championships, 1953–55. In 1956 Geoff was at the centre of a riders' strike in a dispute over money. The sport's governing body, the F.I.M., suspended him for six months and, in his absence, John Surtees won the first of his four 500cc World Championships. After finishing fourth in the 1957 500cc World Championship, he returned to Norton in 1958, claiming third places in both the 350cc and 500c classes.

After finishing fourth in the 500cc World Championship, and fifth in the 350cc class in 1959, he retired. Geoff enjoyed a long retirement before he died on 1 May 2015, aged 92.

Did You Know That?
Geoff Duke was the first racer to compete in a streamlined leather one-piece rather than jacket and trousers.

● 1950 500CC FINAL STANDINGS (TOP 10) ●

Pos	Rider	Nationality	Bike	Pts
1.	Umberto Masetti	(ITA)	Gilera	28
2.	Geoff Duke	(GBR)	Norton	27
3.	Leslie Graham	(GBR)	AJS Porcupine	17
4.	Nello Pagani	(ITA)	Gilera	12
5.	Carlo Bandirola	(ITA)	Gilera	12
6.	Johnny Lockett	(GBR)	Norton	9
7.	Artie Bell	(NIR)	Norton	6
8.	Arcisio Artesiani	(ITA)	MV Agusta	6
9.	Harry Hinton	(AUS)	Norton	5
10.	Ted Friend	(GBR)	AJS	4
=	Dickie Dale	(GBR)	Norton	4
=	Harold Daniell	(GBR)	Norton	4

● CONSTRUCTORS' FINAL STANDINGS (TOP 5) ●

Pos	Team	Nationality	Pts
1.	Norton	(GBR)	28
=	Gilera	(ITA)	28
3.	AJS	(GBR)	21
4.	MV Agusta	(ITA)	6
5.	Triumph	(GBR)	1
=	Velocette	(GBR)	1

● FAST TALK (1) ●

"At the highest level, motorcycle racing is a display of dangerous brilliance; the performance of death-defying feats of skill and daring. That is the underlying contest.
A dance with potential destruction."
Brad Pitt, narrator of Hitting the Apex *(2015),*
written and directed by Mark Neale

● 1951 500CC FINAL STANDINGS (TOP 10) ●

Pos	Rider	Nationality	Bike	Pts
1.	Geoff Duke	(GBR)	Norton	35
2.	Alfredo Milani	(ITA)	Gilera	31
3.	Umberto Masetti	(ITA)	Gilera	21
4.	Bill Doran	(GBR)	AJS	14
5.	Nello Pagani	(ITA)	Gilera	10
6.	Reg Armstrong	(IRL)	AJS	9
7.	Fergus Anderson	(SCO)	Moto Guzzi	8
8.	Enrico Lorenzetti	(ITA)	Norton/Moto Guzzi	8
9.	Tommy Wood	(GBR)	Norton	6
10.	Ken Kavanagh	(AUS)	Norton	6
=	Johnny Lockett	(GBR)	Norton	6

● CONSTRUCTORS' FINAL STANDINGS (TOP 5) ●

Pos	Team	Nationality	Pts
1.	Norton	(GBR)	38
2.	Gilera	(ITA)	36
3.	AJS	(GBR)	21
4.	Moto Guzzi	(ITA)	18
5.	MV Agusta	(ITA)	7

● QUITE A WAIT ●

When Alberto Puig rode his Honda to victory in the 1995 Spanish 500cc Grand Prix, he was the first home rider in 29 GPs to win the race. Home Spanish GP victories at Jerez are now commonplace, with Jorge Lorenzo (three wins), Marc Marquez, Dani Pedroza (two), Sete Gibernau and Alex Criville (three) all taking the chequered flag.

● BRAZIL'S FIRST ●

Brazil has long enjoyed success on four wheels, and in the same year that the nation celebrated its first F1 World Champion, Emerson Fittipaldi, they had seen their first ever rider in a Motorcycle Grand Prix. It was on 7 May 1972 that Adu Celso-Santos (born Eduardo Celso Santos) rode a Yamaha in the 350cc French Grand Prix at Charade, finishing seventh. In 1973, Celso-Santos won his only Grand Prix, taking the chequered flag in the 350cc Spanish Grand Prix at Jarama. He only ever raced in one 500cc Grand Prix, the 1975 West German Grand Prix, also for Yamaha, and he came home ninth.

⚽ GREATEST RACES (1) – 1979 BRITISH GP ⚽

Many fans regard Britain's Barry Sheene's epic battle with American Kenny Roberts in the 1979 British Grand Prix at Silverstone to be the greatest race in MotoGP history. Sheene and Roberts were the two biggest attractions, though defending World Champion Roberts was 28 points clear of the title-winner in 1976 and 1977 (Italy's Virginio Ferrari was only seven behind) with two races remaining.

Roberts claimed pole at a sold-out Silverstone, ahead of Sheene (Suzuki). However, a few minutes before the start, Roberts's Yamaha blew a seal which sprayed oil all over it. Despite this, Roberts – his gloves covered in oil and slipping on the throttle – Sheene and Dutchman Wil Hartog quickly made it a three-man race.

Hartog was dropped, leaving Roberts and Sheene to battle for the lead over the 28 laps. Much to the amusement of the fans, they exchanged hand signals throughout a breathtaking war of attrition between them. It came down to the final lap and Roberts prevailed by a mere 0.3 seconds. Hartog was 4.94 seconds behind Sheene in third, with Ferrari half a minute behind. More importantly, Roberts's second World Championship was all but sealed.

1979 British Grand Prix – Silverstone – Sunday 12 August

Pos	Pts	Rider (Nationality)	Bike	Time/Gap
1.	15	Kenny Roberts (USA)	Yamaha	42m 56.720s
2.	12	Barry Sheene (GBR)	Suzuki	+0.030
3.	10	Wil Hartog (NED)	Suzuki	+4.970
4.	8	Virginio Ferrari (ITA)	Suzuki	+35.280
5.	6	Boet Van Dulmen (NED)	Suzuki	+36.820

Did You Know That?
Barry's famous "V" sign to Kenny was famously misinterpreted as a wave by legendary commentator Murray Walker.

⚽ GOING FISHING ⚽

As Casey Stoner passed the finish line in what he had announced would be his final MotoGP Grand Prix, in Valencia, on 11 November 2012, his Honda mechanics posted a "Going fishing" notice on his pit board. Stoner, who was World Champion in both 2007 (riding for Ducati) and 2011 (for Honda) finished third in the race and third overall in the MotoGP World Championship table. In November 2015, after months of rumours regarding a return to the saddle, Stoner announced he would become a test rider for the Ducati team in 2016.

✦ 1952 500CC FINAL STANDINGS (TOP 10) ✦

Pos	Rider	Nationality	Bike	Pts
1.	Umberto Masetti	(ITA)	Gilera	28
2.	Leslie Graham	(GBR)	MV Agusta	25
3.	Reg Armstrong	(IRL)	Norton	22
4.	Rod Coleman	(NZL)	AJS	15
5.	Jack Brett	(GBR)	AJS/Norton	14
=	Ken Kavanagh	(AUS)	Norton	14
7.	Geoff Duke	(GBR)	Norton	12
=	Nello Pagani	(ITA)	Gilera	12
9.	Cromie McCandless	(NIR)	Norton/Gilera	9
=	Ray Amm	(RHO)	Norton	9

✦ CONSTRUCTORS' FINAL STANDINGS (TOP 5) ✦

Pos	Team	Nationality	Pts
1.	Gilera	(ITA)	39
2.	Norton	(GBR)	36
3.	MV Agusta	(ITA)	33
4.	AJS	(GBR)	22
5.	BMW Agusta	(GER)	1

✦ TWINS OF A DIFFERENT AGE ✦

Casey Stoney's daughter, Alessandra Maria, was born on 16 February 2012. She shares her birthday with a man who was one of her father's biggest rivals in MotoGP, Valentino Rossi.

✦ A BIG WELKOM TO RACE FANS ✦

The Phasika Freeway in Welkom, South Africa, hosted the South African Motorcycle Grand Prix from 1999–2004. The track opened in 1999 and was an exact copy of the Las Vegas Motor Speedway, which had opened its doors two years earlier. The Phasika Freeway accommodates 60,000 spectators and has a 4.24km road course and a 2.4km oval course. The city of Welkom is also known as "Circle City" and "City within a Garden"; Welkom itself is Afrikaans – and Dutch – for welcome.

✦ FAREWELL TOUR ✦

The 1982 season was the last for the 350cc class. The final 350cc World Champion was West Germany's Anton Mang riding for Kawasaki.

● FANTASY 500CC/MOTOGP BRITISH STARTING GRID ●

(to the end of the 2015 season)

1
Mike Hailwood
(76 GP wins, 4
World Championships
1962, 1963, 1964,
1965)

2
John Surtees
(38 GP wins, 4
World Championships
1956, 1958, 1959,
1960)

3
Geoff Duke
(33 GP wins, 4
World Championships
1951, 1953, 1954,
1955)

4
Phil Read
(52 GP wins, 2
World Championships
1973, 1974)

5
Barry Sheene
(23 GP wins, 2
World Championships
1976, 1977)

6
Leslie Graham
(8 GP wins, 1
World Championship
1949)

7
Bill Ivy
(21 GP wins,
125cc World
Champion once)

8
Fergus Anderson
(12 GP wins,
350cc World
Champion twice)

9
Dave Simmonds
(11 GP wins,
125cc World
Champion once)

10
Ralph Bryans
(10 GP wins,
50cc World
Champion once)

● 1953 500CC FINAL STANDINGS (TOP 10) ●

Pos	Rider	Nationality	Bike	Pts
1.	Geoff Duke	(GBR)	Gilera	38
2.	Reg Armstrong	(IRL)	Gilera	24
3.	Alfredo Milani	(ITA)	Gilera	18
=	Ken Kavanagh	(AUS)	Norton/Moto Guzzi	18
5.	Ray Amm	(RHO)	Norton	14
6.	Jack Brett	(GBR)	Norton	13
7.	Dickie Dale	(GBR)	Gilera	11
=	Giuseppe Colnago	(ITA)	Gilera	11
9.	Fergus Anderson	(GBR)	Moto Guzzi	8
10.	Rod Coleman	(NZL)	AJS/Norton	7

● CONSTRUCTORS' FINAL STANDINGS (TOP 5) ●

Pos	Team	Nationality	Pts
1.	Gilera	(ITA)	54
2.	Norton	(GBR)	30
3.	AJS	(GBR)	10
4.	Moto Guzzi	(ITA)	8
=	MV Agusta	(ITA)	8

● ENGLAND DOMINATES ●

All six races in the 1956 500cc Motorcycle World Championship were won by English-born riders. John Surtees, from Talsfield, Surrey, won the first three races, Isle of Man TT, Dutch TT and Belgian GP, for MV Agusta; Scarborough-born John Hartle, on a Norton, won the Ulster GP; Geoff Duke, born in St Helens, won the season-ending Nations GP in Italy for Gilera; and Reg Armstrong, born in Liverpool but raised in Dublin – he represented Ireland – took the German GP, also for Gilera.

● THERE'S NO PLACE LIKE HOME ●

Four of 2015 MotoGP World Champion Jorge Lorenzo's seven victories in the season were at the GPs held in Spain.

● SO NEAR ●

In second practice for the 2013 Italian MotoGP at Mugello, Marc Marquez (Honda), recorded the fastest ever crash on a motorcycle. He came off his bike at 209.9mph (337.9kmh).

❀ MOTOGP BOOKSHELF ❀

There have been many autobiographies by or biographies on motorcycling legends. Here is a selection:

Troy Bayliss	*My Life My Career* (2010)
Alex Criville	*A Life on Wheels* (2010)
Geoff Duke	*In Pursuit of Perfection* (1988)
Jorge Lorenzo	*My Story So Far* (2009)
Marc Marquez	*Dreams Come True – My Story* (2014)
Phil Read	*Prince of Speed* (1970)
Valentino Rossi	*What If I Had Never Tried It* (2006)
Barry Sheene	*Leader of the Pack* (1983)
Casey Stoner	*Pushing the Limits* (2013)
John Surtees	*My Incredible Life on Two and Four Wheels* (2014)

❀ OUT OF THE FRYING PAN? ❀

The ADAC Eifelrennen, organized by the ADAC Automobile Club, was an annual motorsport race held in Germany's Eifel Mountain area from 1922–2003. Early races were on public roads but conditions for the racers became hazardous in wet weather when the unpaved roads became very muddy and slippery. These poor racing conditions led to the construction of the nearby Nurburgring, which was opened in 1927. The Nurburgring, especially the old 14-mile Nordschleife circuit, was also one of the most difficult circuits in all motorsports.

Did You Know That?
The Nurburgring's Nordschleife circuit has Tourist Days when anyone in any vehicle of two or four wheels can complete a lap or more. It attracts thousands of fans every year. One lap in 2016 cost €29, four laps €105, nine laps €220, 25 laps €550. A season ticket cost €1,900.

❀ THE END OF THE 500CC ERA ❀

The 2001 Rio de Janeiro Motorcycle Grand Prix at Autodromo Internacional Nelson Piquet, Rio de Janeiro, Brazil, was the final race of the 2001 season and marked the end of the 500cc era in the sport. The Federation Internationale de Motocyclisme (F.I.M.) agreed to permit 990cc machines to race from season 2002 and the competition was rebranded as MotoGP. Valentino Rossi took the chequered flag for Honda to clinch his first premier-class World Championship title, and he would win the next four world titles too.

● 1954 500CC FINAL STANDINGS (TOP 10) ●

Pos	Rider	Nationality	Bike	Pts
1.	Geoff Duke	(GBR)	Gilera	40
2.	Ray Amm	(RHO)	Norton	20
3.	Ken Kavanagh	(AUS)	Moto Guzzi	16
4.	Dickie Dale	(GBR)	MV Agusta	13
=	Reg Armstrong	(IRL)	Gilera	13
6.	Pierre Moneret	(FRA)	Gilera	8
=	Fergus Anderson	(GBR)	Moto Guzzi	8
=	Carlo Bandirola	(ITA)	MV Agusta	8
=	Jack Brett	(GBR)	Norton	8
10.	Umberto Masetti	(ITA)	Gilera	6
=	Alfredo Milani	(ITA)	Gilera	6

● CONSTRUCTORS' FINAL STANDINGS (TOP 5) ●

Pos	Team	Nationality	Pts
1.	Gilera	(ITA)	54
2.	Norton	(GBR)	29
3.	Moto Guzzi	(ITA)	22
4.	MV Agusta	(ITA)	16
5.	AJS	(GBR)	8

● BRIEF ENCOUNTERS ●

The Motorcycle World Championship visited Brazil 13 times between 1987 and 2004. The first three Grands Prix were at Goiania in 1987–89, and Wayne Gardner (Honda), Eddie Lawson (Yamaha) and Kevin Schwantz (Suzuki), respectively were the winners. In 1992, the race was at Interlagos, where Wayne Rainey on a Yamaha was victorious. In 1995, at the Circuit Nelson Piquet in the Rio de Janeiro suburb of Jacarepagua, the Brazilian Grand Prix returned, and Luca Cadalora brought his Yamaha home in first place. For eight of the next nine years – there was no race in 1998 – the rebranded Rio Grand Prix was staged at Jacarepagua and Valentino Rossi, Honda, won four consecutive races in the 500cc/MotoGP class, 2000–03. Also successful were Michael Doohan, Honda, in 1996 and 1987, Norifumi Abe, Yamaha, in 1999, and Makoto Tamada, Honda, in 2004.

Did You Know That?
The Nelson Piquet Circuit at Jacarepagua was demolished in 2012 in preparation for the 2016 Rio de Janeiro Olympic Games.

⬡ HOMES OF THE FAMOUS BRITISH MARQUES ⬡

Motorcycle manufacturing was a staple of British industry from the late 19th century right up to the late 20th century. These are some of the most famous marques in British motorcycle history:

Company	City	Year Founded
AJS	Wolverhampton	1909
BSA	Gun Quarter, Birmingham	1861
Matchless	Plumstead, London	1899
Metisse	Carswell, Faringdon, Oxfordshire	1969
Norton	Birmingham	1898
Triumph	Meridan, Coventry	1885
Velocette	Hall Green, Birmingham	1904

Did You Know That?
BSA was founded as Birmingham Small Arms Company – hence the address. AJS was A. J. Stevens & Co. AJS was sold to Matchless in 1931, but the name survived until 1969, then was revived in 1974.

⬡ SCOTLAND'S BRAVEHEART ⬡

Alex George was born in Glasgow in March 1949. He began his career in the 250cc class in 1970, riding in two World Championship races, finishing sixth in the Isle of Man TT and fifth in the Ulster GP. It would be three years before he returned to the World Championship stage. George's best season came in the 1975 500cc World Championship when, riding for Yamaha, he finished seventh overall. This was a three-place improvement on his previous best performance – tenth in the 1973 500cc World Championship. Although he did not win a race in any of the 250cc, 350cc or 500cc World Championship classes, he did enjoy three podium finishes all on the bottom step, and was in the top six many times. In 1975, he was third in the 500cc Czech Grand Prix and the 350cc Dutch TT. His final third-place finish came in the 1977 500cc Austrian Grand Prix. George also rode in the F750 class on a 750cc Yamaha. In 1976, George, riding for Honda France (partnered by France's Jean-Claude Mamerin) made his debut in the endurance race, the Bol D'Or at Le Mans, and won it. He enjoyed success in the Isle of Man TT, winning three times, most famously a 3.4 seconds triumph over Mike Hailwood in 1979. However, in the 1982 Isle of Man TT, George had a bad crash in which he suffered serious injuries. Although he made a full recovery, he retired as a regular racer.

◉ 1955 500CC FINAL STANDINGS (TOP 10) ◉

Pos	Rider	Nationality	Bike	Pts
1.	Geoff Duke	(GBR)	Gilera	36
2.	Reg Armstrong	(IRL)	Gilera	30
3.	Umberto Masetti	(ITA)	MV Agusta	19
4.	Giuseppe Calnago	(ITA)	Gilera	13
5.	Carlo Bandirola	(ITA)	MV Agusta	10
6.	Bill Lomas	(GBR)	Moto Guzzi	8
7.	Pierre Moneret	(FRA)	Gilera	6
=	John Hartle	(GBR)	Norton	6
=	Libero Liberati	(ITA)	Gilera	6
=	Walter Zeller	(FRG)	BMW	6

◉ CONSTRUCTORS' FINAL STANDINGS (TOP 5) ◉

Pos	Team	Nationality	Pts
1.	Gilera	(ITA)	54
2.	MV Agusta	(ITA)	25
3.	Moto Guzzi	(ITA)	15
=	Norton	(GBR)	15
5.	BMW	(GER)	7

◉ FAST TALK (2) ◉

"The danger is when one guy puts in danger other guys.
This is the limit."
*Dani Pedrosa referring to Marc Marquez clipping his back wheel
in the 2013 Aragon MotoGP, which caused Pedrosa to crash*

◉ VIVA ESPANA ◉

Spanish riders dominated the 2015 MotoGP World Championship race, with six finishing in the top 12. As well as champion Jorge Lorenzo, Marc Marquez was third, Dani Pedrosa finished fourth, Pol Espargaro came ninth, his brother Aleix took 11th, one place ahead of top rookie Maverick Vinales. Of the 18 races in 2015, 14 were won by Spanish riders with Rossi taking the other four. Spain also dominated the MotoGP calendar too, because there were four races in the country: the Spanish GP at Jerez, the Catalan GP at the Circuit Catalunya (just outside Barcelona), the Aragon GP at Alcaniz, in north-east Spain, and the season-ending Valencian GP on a street circuit in the city of Valencia.

❂ THEY'VE GOT IT LICKED ❂

To commemorate Japanese manufacturer Honda's 50 years of competing at the Isle of Max TT series in 2009, the Isle of Man Post Office issued a set of commemorative stamps. Each stamp featured a legendary rider spanning six decades in which Honda motorcycles have raced at the TT: Naomi Taniguchi (1950s), Mike Hailwood (1960s), Alex George (1970s), Joey Dunlop (1980s), Steve Hislop (1990s) and, at the date of issue, the 14-times TT winner John McGuinness (2000s).

❂ ITALIAN TRIO PARK THEIR BIKES ❂

At the end of the 1957 season, three Italian works teams left the Grand Prix scene, Gilera, Mondial and Moto Guzzi, and all went out with the World Champions riding their motorcycles. The 250cc World Champion was Britain's Cecil Stanford and he had two Mondial team-mates just beneath him in the table, Italy's Tarquinio Provini – in second – and compatriot Sammy Miller in third. Moto Guzzi provided the World Champion in the 350cc class, with Australia's Keith Campbell beating a pair of Gilera riders, Bob McIntyre and Libero Liberati, into second and third place, respectively. The Italian Liberati would not be denied, however, in the 500cc World Championship, again ahead of British Gilera team-mate McIntyre. The last Grand Prix for the three Italian marques was on home soil, the Nations GP at Monza and Mondial (through Provini in the 250cc race) and Gilera (McIntyre in the 350cc and Liberati in the 500cc races) both went out winners. All three teams cited escalating costs as their reasons for leaving the World Championship and many fans and commentators believe 1957 signalled the end of the golden age of the Motorcycle World Championship.

❂ ENGLAND DOMINATES ❂

There was a major change in the garages of motorcycle racing in the World Championship for its 50th season. From 1998, all 500cc motorbikes had to race on unleaded fuel. Honda's Mick Doohan was the first unleaded 500cc World Champion.

Did You Know That?
The main difference between leaded petrol and unleaded petrol is the additive tetraethyl lead.

❂ JOHN SURTEES – KING ON 2- AND 4-WHEELS ❂

John Surtees MBE, OBE, CBE, was born on 11 February 1934, the son of a South London motorcycle dealer. His racing debut was in the sidecar of his father's Vincent motorbike, a race the pair won, but when officials discovered John was 14, the Surteeses were disqualified. At 15, John entered his first race in a grasstrack competition and, in 1951, the motorcycle racing world discovered his potential when he gave Geoff Duke, reigning 350cc and 500cc Motorcycle World Champion, a strong challenge in an Auto-Cycle Union (ACU) race at Thruxton in England.

In 1955, Norton boss Joe Craig gambled and offered 21-year-old John his first sponsored bike to race in 350cc and 500cc World Championship events. Although he finished sixth in the 350cc World Championship, and scored no points in three races in the elite class, John did win the 250cc Ulster Grand Prix riding for German team NSU. At the end of that season, Norton were in financial difficulty and Surtees was snapped up by the Italian MV Agusta factory outfit for 1956. The 500cc World Championship featured a six-race calendar and John won the first three, on his way to becoming World Champion. It was MV Agusta's first 500cc win and John was nicknamed Figlio del Vento – "Son of the Wind". Gilera was too powerful for MV Agusta in 1957, winning five of the six races. John did win the Dutch TT and finished third in the 500cc World Championship. Gilera's (and Moto Guzzi's) shock decision to pull out of racing in 1958 paved the way for John and MV Agusta to dominate the 350cc and 500cc World Championship for three years.

John won all six races he entered in both classes to be crowned dual 1958 World Champion. It was the same story in 1959 as he won every race he entered, six in the 350cc category and seven in 500cc. The following season he was not as dominant in the saddle as previously but still managed to achieve an unprecedented treble in consecutive years by winning the 350cc and 500cc World Championship titles. Quite remarkably, or perhaps not, John won 32 out of the 36 races he started between 1958 and 1960.

What makes John's third double World Championship even more remarkable is that, in 1960, in addition to riding in seven Motorcycle World Championship Grands Prix, he drove in four Formula 1 GPs, too. Driving for Colin Chapman's Lotus team, he retired from the Monaco, Portuguese and American Grands Prix, but finished second in the British Grand Prix and those six points were good enough for 14th place in that World Championship table. The switch from two wheels to four was made permanent in 1961 and for 12 seasons, until 1972, he was a motor racing driver. In 1963, John joined Ferrari and won the 1964 Formula One World Championship.

Also in 1964, John and Ferrari team-mate Lorenzo Bandini took third place in the Le Mans 24 Hours Race. One of the most talented and versatile racers ever, John, the only World Champion in the two- and four-wheel elite class, ran his own F1 team 1970–78. In the 2016 New Year's Honours List, John was made a CBE to add to his MBE and OBE.

Did You Know That?
John was the first racer to win the Senior TT at the Isle of Man three years in succession, 1958, 1959 and 1960.

● 1956 500CC FINAL STANDINGS (TOP 10) ●

Pos	Rider	Nationality	Bike	Pts
1.	John Surtees	(GBR)	MV Agusta	24
2.	Walter Zeller	(FRG)	BMW	16
3.	John Hartle	(GBR)	Norton	14
4.	Pierre Moneret	(FRA)	Gilera	12
5.	Reg Armstrong	(IRL)	Gilera	11
6.	Umberto Masetti	(ITA)	MV Agusta	9
7.	Geoff Duke	(GBR)	Gilera	8
8.	Bob Brown	(AUS)	Matchless	6
=	Libero Liberati	(ITA)	Gilera	6
=	Eddie Grant	(RSA)	Norton	6

● CONSTRUCTORS' FINAL STANDINGS (TOP 5) ●

Pos	Team	Nationality	Pts
1.	MV Agusta	(ITA)	32
2.	Gilera	(ITA)	20
3.	Norton	(GBR)	21
4.	BMW	(GER)	19
5.	Matchless	(GBR)	9

● ONCE WAS RARELY ENOUGH ●

The 50cc World Championship ran for 22 years, 1962–83, succeeded by an 80cc event for six years, 1984–89. Almost every World Champion in these classes enjoyed more than one title. In fact, only Ernst Degner of Germany, in 1962, Britain's Ralph Bryan, in 1965, Dutchman Hans Van Kessel, in 1974, and the last winner Manuel Herros did not add to their first World Championship. Stefan Dorflinger won four straight titles, two each in the 50cc and 80cc classes.

❀ ALL-TIME MOTOGP WORLD CHAMPIONS ❀

There have been 27 500cc/MotoGP World Champions since the inaugural season in 1949. This is the full list:

Year	Rider	Year	Rider
1949	Leslie Graham	1983	Freddie Spencer
1950	Umberto Masetti	1984	Eddie Lawson
1951	Geoff Duke	1985	Freddie Spencer
1952	Umberto Masetti	1986	Eddie Lawson
1953	Geoff Duke	1987	Wayne Gardner
1954	Geoff Duke	1988	Eddie Lawson
1955	Geoff Duke	1989	Eddie Lawson
1956	John Surtees	1990	Wayne Rainey
1957	Libero Liberati	1991	Wayne Rainey
1958	John Surtees	1992	Wayne Rainey
1959	John Surtees	1993	Kevin Schwantz
1960	John Surtees	1994	Mick Doohan
1961	Gary Hocking	1995	Mick Doohan
1962	Mike Hailwood	1996	Mick Doohan
1963	Mike Hailwood	1997	Mick Doohan
1964	Mike Hailwood	1998	Mick Doohan
1965	Mike Hailwood	1999	Alex Criville
1966	Giacomo Agostini	2000	Kenny Roberts Jr
1967	Giacomo Agostini	2001	Valentino Rossi
1968	Giacomo Agostini	2002	Valentino Rossi
1969	Giacomo Agostini	2003	Valentino Rossi
1970	Giacomo Agostini	2004	Valentino Rossi
1971	Giacomo Agostini	2005	Valentino Rossi
1972	Giacomo Agostini	2006	Nicky Hayden
1973	Phil Read	2007	Casey Stoner
1974	Phil Read	2008	Valentino Rossi
1975	Giacomo Agostini	2009	Valentino Rossi
1976	Barry Sheene	2010	Jorge Lorenzo
1977	Barry Sheene	2011	Casey Stoner
1978	Kenny Roberts	2012	Jorge Lorenzo
1979	Kenny Roberts	2013	Marc Marquez
1980	Kenny Roberts	2014	Marc Marquez
1981	Marco Lucchinelli	2015	Jorge Lorenzo
1982	Franco Uncini		

Did You Know That?
The 27 World Champions have come from only six countries.

❀ JAPAN'S FIRST STEPS ❀

Japanese motor giants Honda entered the world of motorcycle racing at the 1959 Isle of Man TT Series. Five riders came over and Naomi Taniguchi became the first Japanese racer to win a point in the F.I.M. World Championship when Honda entered him in the 125cc race over the Clypse course. Taniguchi came in sixth, Giichi Suzuki seventh, Teisuke Tanaka eighth and Junzo Suzuki tenth. Unfortunately, the fifth Honda rider, an American Bill Hunt (as well as being a racer, he was the Honda team's translator) had to retire after a crash. Taniguchi received a silver replica trophy, Giichi Suzuki and Tanaka bronze replicas, and the Honda team won the Constructors' Prize. Taniguchi's best season was 1960 when he finished tenth in the 125cc World Championship for Honda.

❀ CONFUSED PARENTAGE ❀

Ducati is a hugely successful Italian motorcycle manufacturer, based in Bologna. However, Ducati is, in fact, owned by Germans, Audi, through Audi's Italian subsidiary, Lamborghini. The famous Italian marque, however, was owned another by German car giant, Volkswagen.

❀ KING KENNY GETS A NEW TOY ❀

Three-time 500cc World Champion Kenny Roberts (Sr) began the 1982 season by winning the Argentine 500cc Grand Prix, riding the previous year's square-four cylinder Yamaha. For the next race, the Austrian GP, Yamaha's OW61 YZR600 V4-engined bike was ready and Roberts rode it to third place. Next time out, in the Spanish GP at Jarama, he won the race, beating Yamaha team-mate Barry Sheene. Injuries curtailed Roberts's season and he finished fourth in the 500cc World Championship with Franco Uncini of Italy on top.

Did You Know That?
Kenny was the first American to win the 500cc World Championship in 1978, but between 1983 and 1993, 10 titles went to Americans.

❀ IT'S NOT HOW YOU START ... ❀

Despite not winning a point in the first two rounds, Marco Simoncelli went on to win the 250cc World Championship, the first for Gilera.

❂ 1957 500CC FINAL STANDINGS (TOP 10) ❂

Pos	Rider	Nationality	Bike	Pts
1.	Libero Liberati	(ITA)	Gilera	32
2.	Bob McIntyre	(GBR)	Gilera	20
3.	John Surtees	(GBR)	MV Agusta	17
4.	Geoff Duke	(GBR)	Gilera	10
5.	Jack Brett	(GBR)	Norton	9
6.	Walter Zeller	(FRG)	BMW	8
7.	Keith Bryen	(AUS)	Matchless/Norton/ Moto Guzzi	7
8.	Dickie Dale	(GBR)	Moto Guzzi	6
9.	Alfredo Milani	(ITA)	Gilera	4
=	Bob Brown	(AUS)	Gilera	4
=	Terry Shepherd	(GBR)	MV Agusta	4

❂ CONSTRUCTORS' FINAL STANDINGS (TOP 5) ❂

Pos	Team	Nationality	Pts
1.	Gilera	(ITA)	46
2.	MV Agusta	(ITA)	20
3.	Norton	(GBR)	13
4.	BMW	(GER)	9
5.	Moto Guzzi	(ITA)	8

❂ CHAS MORTIMER'S DAY IN THE SUN ❂

Giacomo Agostini dominated the 1972 500cc World Championship, winning 11 of the first 12 races. He retired from the Yugoslav Grand Prix, the sixth race, giving compatriot and MV Agusta team-mate Alberto Pagani victory – the third and last of his career. Agostini did not compete at the season-ending Spanish GP at Montjuich, and the victory went to a British rider, Chas Mortimer, who gave Yamaha their first victory in a 500cc World Championship race. Mortimer won F.I.M. World Championship races at 125cc, 250cc, 350cc, 500cc – this was his only one – and 750cc, the only man to achieve this feat.

❂ STAMP OF CLASS ❂

When Australian Kel Carruthers won the 1969 250cc World Championship, the Mutawakelite Kingdom of Yemen (now part of the Kingdom of Yemen) issued a stamp with his image on it. Carruthers remains the only Australian ever to be the 250cc World Champion.

⬤ GREATEST RACES (2) – 1992 HUNGARIAN GP ⬤

America's Wayne Rainey (Yamaha) trailed the Australian Mick Doohan (Honda) by 75 points after seven rounds of the 1992 500cc World Championship. Sadly Doohan suffered a terrible injury in practice for round eight. However, for round nine, it was a canny veteran who stole the show at the Hungarian GP, thanks to heavy rain at the Hungaroring.

Every rider, except for American Eddie Lawson – a four-time 500cc World Champion – started on full wet tyres. "Steady Eddie" gambled on the track drying, so put slicks on his Cagiva Corse. The weather first deteriorated, however, causing stewards to suspend the race.

Lawson's gamble paid dividends after the resumption because, while others changed their rubber for the now drying track, he cut through the field. He overtook Kevin Schwantz (Suzuki) for fourth place, then passed Rainey and Randy Mamola (Yamaha). With two laps remaining, Lawson flew past Doug Chandler (Suzuki) and pulled away to give Cagiva its first 500cc win. It was Lawson's 31st and final 500cc victory of his career. Rainey, who finished fifth, went on to retain his world title by four points from Doohan.

1992 Hungarian Grand Prix – Hungaroring – Sunday 12 July

Pos	Pts	Rider (Nationality)	Bike	Time/Gap
1.	20	Eddie Lawson (USA)	Cagiva	57m 21.786s
2.	15	Doug Chandler (USA)	Suzuki	+14.194s
3.	12	Randy Mamola (USA)	Yamaha	+37.730s
4.	10	Kevin Schwantz (USA)	Suzuki	+1m 03.608s
5.	8	Wayne Rainey (USA)	Yamaha	+1m 07.662s

Did You Know That?

The Hungaroring Circuit hosted the first Formula One Grand Prix to be held behind the Iron Curtain in 1986. It was also the first Hungarian GP for 50 years.

⬤ A VERY BRIEF VISIT ⬤

Barry Sheene made his one and only appearance at the Isle of Man TT in 1971. The weather conditions for the 125cc race were appalling and, on Lap 2, Sheene's Suzuki slipped at Quarterbridge and he decided to retire from the race. Although known as one of the bravest and fastest riders in motorcycle racing history, Sheene, throughout his career, was a vociferous opponent of the Isle of Man TT being part of the F.I.M. World Championship.

● 1958 500CC FINAL STANDINGS (TOP 10) ●

Pos	Rider	Nationality	Bike	Pts
1.	John Surtees	(GBR)	MV Agusta	32
2.	John Hartle	(GBR)	MV Agusta	20
3.	Geoff Duke	(GBR)	BMW/Norton	13
=	Dickie Dale	(GBR)	BMW	13
5.	Derek Minter	(GBR)	Norton	10
6.	Gary Hocking	(RHO)	Norton	8
=	Ernst Hiller	(FRG)	BMW	8
8.	Bob Anderson	(GBR)	Norton	7
9.	Keith Campbell	(AUS)	Norton	6
=	Bob McIntyre	(GBR)	Norton	6
=	Remo Venturi	(ITA)	MV Agusta	6
=	Bob Brown	(AUS)	Norton/BMW	6

● CONSTRUCTORS' FINAL STANDINGS (TOP 3) ●

Pos	Team	Nationality	Pts
1.	MV Agusta	(ITA)	48
2.	Norton	(GBR)	35
3.	BMW	(GER)	19

● FAST TALK (3) ●

"Broken femur, collarbone and ribs, busted wrists and forearm,
and a lot of skin off in the wrong places. Other than that,
I feel brand new."
*Barry Sheene lying in his hospital bed after crashing
at 170mph in the 1975 Daytona 200*

● HONOURED BY THE QUEEN ●

These motorcycle racers have been honoured by HM The Queen:

Geoff Duke	OBE
Mike Hailwood	MBE, George Medal
John Surtees	MBE, OBE, CBE
Joey Dunlop	MBE
Jim Redmond	MBE
Phil Read	MBE
Barry Sheene	MBE
Mick Doohan	Order of Australia
Casey Stoner	Order of Australia

● MARCO SIMONCELLI ●

The Sepang International Circuit, at Sepang, Selangor, Malaysia has an acronym, SIC. Sic, coincidentally, was Marco Simoncelli's nickname and the circuit was a home from home for the Italian rider as tens of thousands of fans flocked to the track, just to watch him race. Whenever he competed there, no matter where you looked, there would be thousands of flags bearing his image, his nickname and his number, 58. Hugely popular on and off the track, Marco's greatest and worst moments in his motorcycling career happened at the Malaysian circuit.

On 19 October 2008, he clinched the 250cc World Championship for Gilera with one race to go. Four years later, on 23 October 2011, riding a Honda in the Malaysian Grand Prix, at turn 11 of the second lap, Marco was involved in a collision. Simoncelli's helmet was ripped off in the accident and he lay motionless on the track. He was rushed by ambulance to the circuit's medical centre but less than one hour after the collision Marco died. It was the first fatality in MotoGP since Japan's Daijiro Katoh died from injuries sustained at the 2003 Japanese Grand Prix.

Marco's World Championship career statistics are as follows:

Year	Category	Manufacturer	Starts	Points	Wins	Rank
2002	125cc	Aprilia	6	3	–	33rd
2003	125cc	Aprilia	15	31	–	21st
2004	125cc	Aprilia	13	79	1	11th
2005	125cc	Aprilia	16	177	1	5th
2006	250cc	Gilera	16	92	–	10th
2007	250cc	Gilera	17	97	–	10th
2008	250cc	Gilera	16	281	6	1st
2009	250cc	Gilera	15	231	6	3rd
2010	MotoGP	Honda	18	125		8th
2011	MotoGP	Honda	16	139	–	6th

Marco's MotoGP firsts:

First race: Qatar GP, Doha, 11 April 2010
First points: Qatar GP, Doha, 11 April 2010, 5 points (11th)
First pole: Spanish GP, Circuit de Catalunya, 5 June 2011
First podium: 3rd place, Czech Republic GP, Brno, 14 August 2011
Best finish: 2nd place, Australian GP, Philip Island, 16 Oct 2011

⚙ 1959 500CC FINAL STANDINGS (TOP 10) ⚙

Pos	Rider (Nationality)	Bike	Pts
1.	John Surtees (GBR)	MV Agusta	32
2.	Remo Venturi (ITA)	MV Agusta	20
3.	Bob Brown (AUS)	Norton	13
4.	Geoff Duke (GBR)	Norton	13
5.	Gary Hocking (RHO)	Norton	10
6.	Bob McIntyre (GBR)	Norton	8
7.	Alistair King (GBR)	Norton	8
8.	Dickie Dale (GBR)	BMW	7
9.	Terry Shepherd (GBR)	Norton	6
10.	John Hempleman (NZL)	Norton	6

⚙ CONSTRUCTORS' FINAL STANDINGS (TOP 4) ⚙

Pos	Team	Nationality	Pts
1.	MV Agusta	(ITA)	56
2.	Norton	(GBR)	36
3.	BMW	(GER)	7
4.	Matchless	(GBR)	3

⚙ A CLASS ACT IN EVERY CATEGORY ⚙

In an 18-year career 1972–89, Swiss rider Bruno Kneubuhler competed in every World Championship Grand Prix class from 50cc to 500cc, but was never a World Champion. He made his debut in 1972, riding for Yamaha in both the 500cc and 350cc World Championship and managed a win in the season-ending 350cc Spanish Grand Prix and two third-place finishes and overall third place in the 500cc class. His ability to get the maximum out of any machine was most evident in the 1973 Spanish GP, finishing in the 50cc (on a Kreidler), 250cc (Yamaha) and 500cc (Yamaha) races. Kneubuhler won three 125cc GPs, one each in 50cc and 350cc races, and claimed a podium finish 33 times. He was a World Championship runner-up on three occasions: 50cc for Kriedler in 1973, 125cc for Yamaha in 1974 and 125cc for MBA in 1983.

Did You Know That?

On 29 June 1974, at the Dutch TT at Assen, Harley Davidson rider Walter Villa won the 250cc race, 43.6 seconds clear of Bruno Kneubuhler, riding a Yamaha. A mere 0.6 seconds behind the Swiss rider was another Yamaha, this one ridden by a 22-year-old American, making his World Championship debut, Kenny Roberts.

❖ MENTORING A FUTURE KING ❖

Australia's Kel Carruthers, riding for Benelli, was the 1969 250cc World Champion. Influenced by his father, a motorcyle show owner, he learned to ride bikes at a very young age. After the Australian 125cc, 250cc, 350cc and 500cc National Championships, he moved to Europe in 1966 and raced in his first World Championship season that year for Honda (125cc) and Norton (350cc and 500cc). In all, Carruthers won seven World Championship-counting Grands Prix, all in the 125cc class. No win was more crucial than the 1969 season-ending Yugoslav GP. The 125cc World Championship was Spain's Ossa rider Santiago Herrero's to lose, as he needed only a top-two finish; Kent Andersson from Sweden, on a Yamaha, if Herrero finished off the podium, needed to beat Carruthers. Instead, Carruthers won, Andersson was third and Herraro fifth, giving the Australian the title by five points from the Swede and six from the Spaniard.

After the 1970 season Carruthers accepted an offer from Yamaha to race in North America and become a mentor to an up-and-coming young dirt track racer, Kenny Roberts. Carruthers became manager of Yamaha's American racing team in 1973 and, under his tutelage, Roberts won the 1973 and 1974 Grand National Championship. Yamaha sent Roberts, under Carruthers's management, to Europe to compete in the 1978 Motorcycle World Championship. It was a masterful decision as Roberts won the 500cc World Championship in his debut season and retained the title in 1979 and 1980. Carruthers later managed Eddie Lawson to one of his three 500cc World Championships. He was inducted into the Sport Australia Hall of Fame in 1985, and into the AMA Motorcycle Hall of Fame in 1999.

❖ CAUGHT ON CAMERA ❖

Like many motorcycle racers of his era, Canada's Mike Duff competed in various classes every season. His career was a relatively short one, from 1961 to 1967, during which time he won three times, though never in the 500cc category. In 1965, while testing in Japan, Duff suffered life-threatening injuries in a crash. The story of his recovery was documented by the National Film Board of Canada in 1967 in a short film called *Ride for Your Life*, directed by Robin Spy.

❖ LESS THAN THE BLINK OF AN EYE ❖

MotoGP timings are now measured in thousandths of a second. At 200kph, a motorbike covers 5.5cm (2.16 inches) in 0.001 of a second.

❀ 1960 500CC FINAL STANDINGS (TOP 10) ❀

Pos	Rider	Nationality	Bike	Pts
1.	John Surtees	(GBR)	MV Agusta	32
2.	Remo Venturi	(ITA)	MV Agusta	26
3.	John Hartle	(GBR)	MV Agusta/Norton	16
4.	Bob Brown	(AUS)	Norton	15
=	Emilio Mendogni	(ITA)	MV Agusta	15
6.	Mike Hailwood	(GBR)	Norton	13
7.	Paddy Driver	(RSA)	Norton	9
8.	Dickie Dale	(GBR)	BMW	6
9.	Jim Redman	(Rhodesia)	Norton	5
10.	Alan Shepherd	(GBR)	Matchless	4
=	Tom Phillis	(AUS)	Norton	4

❀ CONSTRUCTORS' FINAL STANDINGS (TOP 4) ❀

Pos	Team	Nationality	Pts
1.	MV Agusta	(ITA)	54
2.	Norton	(GBR)	33
3.	Matchless	(GBR)	4
4.	BMW	(GER)	1

❀ TOURIST TROPHY ❀

The Isle of Man TT was, *de facto*, the British Grand Prix from 1949, the first year of the Motorcycle World Championship, until 1976. From 1977 the Manx streets were replaced by the former runway at Silverstone in Northamptonshire, the long-time home of Formula 1 motor racing's British Grand Prix. This was not the end of Tourist Trophy races in the World Championship because the race in the Netherlands, at Assen, is also a TT event and not a Grand Prix.

Did You Know That?
As would be the case with F1's first ever World Championship race in 1950, the F.I.M. World Championship's inaugural race, in 1949, was in the British Isles, the Tourist Trophy on the Isle of Man.

❀ GETTING CLOSER ❀

Two Britons, Bradley Smith (sixth) and Cal Crutchlow (eighth), were in 2015's MotoGP World Championship top eight for the first time since Niall MacKenzie was seventh and Ron Haslam eighth in 1989.

● FANTASY 500CC/MOTOGP
ITALIAN STARTING GRID ●

(to the end of the 2015 season)

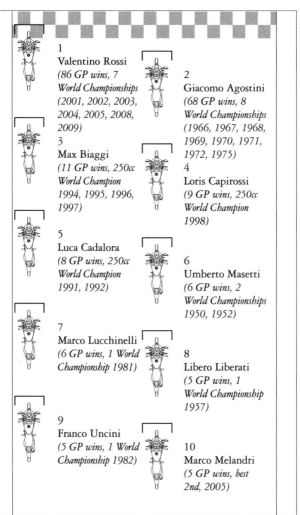

1
Valentino Rossi
(86 GP wins, 7
World Championships
(2001, 2002, 2003,
2004, 2005, 2008,
2009)

2
Giacomo Agostini
(68 GP wins, 8
World Championships
(1966, 1967, 1968,
1969, 1970, 1971,
1972, 1975)

3
Max Biaggi
(11 GP wins, 250cc
World Champion
1994, 1995, 1996,
1997)

4
Loris Capirossi
(9 GP wins, 250cc
World Champion
1998)

5
Luca Cadalora
(8 GP wins, 250cc
World Champion
1991, 1992)

6
Umberto Masetti
(6 GP wins, 2
World Championships
1950, 1952)

7
Marco Lucchinelli
(6 GP wins, 1 World
Championship 1981)

8
Libero Liberati
(5 GP wins, 1
World Championship
1957)

9
Franco Uncini
(5 GP wins, 1 World
Championship 1982)

10
Marco Melandri
(5 GP wins, best
2nd, 2005)

❀ MIKE HAILWOOD MBE, GM – MIKE THE BIKE ❀

Stanley Michael Bailey (Mike) Hailwood is regarded by many motorcycle racing experts to be the greatest rider in the sport's history. His innate ability earned him the nickname, "Mike The Bike". The son of a racer and owner of a motorcycle dealership, Mike was born on 2 April 1940 in Oxfordshire. He watched his first motorcycle race aged 10, and was 16 when he went to his first Isle of Man TT meeting. There he watched John Surtees win the 500cc race on his way to the first of his four 500cc World Championships.

Mike was 20 days past his 17th birthday when he first competed, finishing 11th in a race at Oulton Park. He won the 1958 Pinhard Prize – awarded to the young (under 21) rider of the year. He continued to impress in both 1959 and 1960, which led, in 1961, to him signing for Japanese factory team, Honda. Mike repaid their faith in him by winning four Grands Prix, including the Isle of Man Lightweight TT, and the 250cc World Championship. No rider had ever won three TT races on the Snaefell course in the same year, until Mike, who also won the 125cc Lightweight and 500cc Senior classes.

MV Agusta, the most successful manufacturer of the era, signed Mike in 1962. It was a shrewd move by the Italian giants as Mike went on to win four consecutive 500cc World Championships, 1962–65, the first rider to do so. Not content with bikes, Mike drove Formula One cars for Reg Parnell Racing between 1963 and 1965. In 1966, he returned to Honda and won four more World Championships, the 250cc and 350cc double in 1966 and 1967. Awarded the MBE in 1968, the following year Mike swapped handlebars for a steering wheel, finishing third in the 1969 Le Mans 24-Hour and third in the Formula 5000 Championship. He returned to motorbikes in 1970, lured back by BSA, and rode a Rocket 3 in the Daytona 200 in 1970 and 1971.

In 1971, John Surtees signed Mike to drive for his Formula One team. On the second lap of the 1973 South African Grand Prix at Kyalami, Mike collided with Clay Regazzoni, whose BRM burst into flames. Having no regard for his own safety, Mike pulled the trapped and unconscious Regazzoni out of his blazing wreckage, despite his own suit catching fire. This act of heroism was rewarded with the George Medal for civilian gallantry. In an eerie coincidence, Mike was forced to retire from Formula One after suffering severe injuries in the 1974 German Grand Prix – the race was won by Regazzoni, who had recovered from his injuries a year earlier.

On 3 June 1978, 11 years after his last competitive ride, Mike returned to the Isle of Man TT. Although 38, his steely determination came through and he won his 13th Isle of Man TT race. In 1979, he won his last ever TT, the Senior Race, riding a Suzuki RG500. Aged 39, he retired for good.

Tragically on 21 March 1981, he was involved in a car crash, in which his nine-year-old daughter, Michelle, died instantly. Mike and his son, David, were taken to hospital, but Mike died two days later.

Did You Know That?
At the 1978 Isle of Man TT, a large poster on a wall in Douglas read "Hailwood Chooses Castrol." Someone scored out Hailwood and replaced it with "God Chooses Castrol."

❀ 1961 500CC FINAL STANDINGS (TOP 10) ❀

Pos	Rider	Nationality	Bike	Pts
1.	Gary Hocking	(RHO)	MV Agusta	48
2.	Mike Hailwood	(GBR)	Norton/MV Agusta	40
3.	Frank Perris	(GBR)	Norton	16
4.	Bob McIntyre	(SCO)	Norton	14
5.	Alistair King	(SCO)	Norton	13
6.	Bert Schneider	(AUS)	Matchless	9
7.	Jorge Kissling	(ARG)	Matchless	8
8.	Ron Kingston	(GBR)	Matchless	7
9.	Juan Carlos Salatino	(ARG)	Norton	6
10.	Paddy Driver	(RSA)	Norton	5
=	Mike Duff	(CAN)	Matchless	5

❀ CONSTRUCTORS' FINAL STANDINGS (TOP 4) ❀

Pos	Team	Nationality	Pts
1.	MV Agusta	(ITA)	64
2.	Norton	(GBR)	60
3.	Matchless	(GBR)	20
4.	BMW	(GER)	4

❀ BROTHERS AND RIVALS ❀

Sibling rivalry is common in sports, and MotoGP has a pair of top 10 brothers. Pol, the 2013 Moto2 World Champion, and Aleix Espargaro, from Granollers in Spain, finished six and seventh in the 2014 MotoGP World Championship. Aleix, born on 30 July 1989, is almost two years older than Pol, born on 10 June 1991.

⬢ 1962 500CC FINAL STANDINGS (TOP 10) ⬢

Pos	Rider	Nationality	Bike	Pts
1.	Mike Hailwood	(GBR)	MV Agusta	40
2.	Alan Shepherd	(GBR)	Matchless	29
3.	Phil Read	(GBR)	Norton	11
4.	Bert Schneider	(AUS)	Norton	10
5.	Benedicto Caldarella	(ARG)	Matchless	8
=	Gary Hocking	(RHO)	MV Agusta	8
7.	Frantisek Stastny	(TCH)	Jawa	7
8.	Tony Godfrey	(GBR)	Norton	7
9.	Paddy Driver	(RSA)	Norton	7
10.	Sven-Olof Gunnarsson	(SWE)	Norton	6
=	Derek Minter	(GBR)	Norton	6
=	Ellis Boyce	(GBR)	Norton/Matchless	6
=	Juan Carlos Salatino	(ARG)	Norton	6
=	Remo Venturi	(ITA)	MV Agusta	6

⬢ CONSTRUCTORS' FINAL STANDINGS (TOP 5) ⬢

Pos	Team	Nationality	Pts
1.	MV Agusta	(ITA)	48
2.	Norton	(GBR)	39
3.	Matchless	(GBR)	37
4.	Jawa	(CZE)	7
5.	Bianchi	(ITA)	4

⬢ SILVERSTONE'S CORNERS ⬢

Silverstone, an airfield in World War 2, has hosted the British Motorcycling Grand Prix since 1977. These are the track's corners:

Abbey ❖ Farm ❖ Village ❖ The Loop ❖ Brooklands ❖ Luffield ❖ Woodcote ❖ Copse ❖ Maggots ❖ Aintree ❖ Becketts ❖ Chapel ❖ Stowe ❖ Club

Did You Know That?
The Silverstone straights include Wellington, Hanger and Vale.

⬢ YOU NEVER LOSE IT ⬢

Alex George was 43 years old when he rode in the 1992 Isle of Man Senior Manx TT. He finished 11th on a 500cc Manx Norton.

❀ ROSSI'S RECORD RUN OF STARTS OVERTAKEN ❀

At the 2015 German Grand Prix, Italian rider, Andrea Dovizioso, equalled Valentino Rossi's record for an unbroken sequence of Grand Prix starts with 230. Rossi did not miss a single race between his Grand Prix debut at the 1996 125cc Malaysian Grand Prix – he finished sixth on an Aprilia – until he was forced to withdraw from the 2010 MotoGP Italian Grand Prix at Mugello after breaking his right leg in a crash during practice. Dovizioso made his Grand Prix debut at Mugello in the 125cc 2001 Italian Grand Prix, also riding for Aprilia before joining the racing circuit as a full-time rider for Honda in 1992. Despite having to retire after Lap 14 of the German Grand Prix following an accident, Dovizioso was back on his Ducati Desmosedici GP15 for the next race, the Indianapolis Grand Prix, and surpassed Rossi's total.

❀ SIDECAR CHAMPIONSHIPS ❀

The Sidecar World Championship moved from the F.I.M.'s auspices in 1997 and became part of the World Superbikes Championship series. However, since then, the competition has been rebranded a number of times and been regulated by a number of bodies. These are the various titles since 1997:

Title	Years
Sidecar World Cup	1997–2000
Superside	2001–03
Superside World Cup	2004
Superside	2005–09
Superside Sidecar World Championship	2010–15

Did You Know That?
In 2014 and 2015, there was a second, junior, Superside Sidecar World Championship competition, the Sidecar F2 World Championship.

❀ A UNQUE DOUBLE ❀

On 21 July 2013, at the USA MotoGP at Leguna Seca, California, Marc Marquez (Honda) became the first racer to win on his debut at the circuit. Having won the previous race, the German Grand Prix at the Sachsenring, he became the youngest rider to win back-to-back Grand Prix races in the sport's premier class.

◉ 1963 500CC FINAL STANDINGS (TOP 10) ◉

Pos	Rider	Nationality	Bike	Pts
1.	Mike Hailwood	(GBR)	MV Agusta	40
2.	Alan Shepherd	(GBR)	Matchless	21
3.	John Hartle	(GBR)	Gilera	20
4.	Phil Read	(GBR)	Gilera	16
5.	Fred Stevens	(GBR)	Norton	13
6.	Mike Duff	(CAN)	Matchless	11
7.	Derek Minter	(GBR)	Gilera	10
8.	Jack Findlay	(AUS)	Matchless	8
9.	Jorge Kissling	(ARG)	Norton	6
10.	Jack Ahearn	(GBR)	Norton	5

◉ CONSTRUCTORS' FINAL STANDINGS (TOP 5) ◉

Pos	Team	Nationality	Pts
1.	MV Agusta	(ITA)	56
2.	Matchless	(GBR)	34
3.	Gilera	(ITA)	32
4.	Norton	(GER)	24
5.	CKEB	(URS)	1

◉ FAST TALK (4) ◉

"If you believe you are the best, you can't get better,
and I always want to get better."
Valentino Rossi

◉ MAKE HASTE SLOWLY ◉

Michael "Mike" Alan Duff was born in Toronto, Canada, on 13 December 1959 and competed in the Motorcycle Road Racing World Championships from 1960–67, racing in all four classes, 125cc, 250cc, 350cc and 500cc. His career highlights were a fourth-place finish in the 1964 500cc World Championship, victory in the 1965 250cc Finnish Grand Prix, and he was runner-up to Phil Read in that year's 250cc World Championship. In 1984, Michael Alan Duff, who once said that he felt like he was "wearing the shoes on the wrong feet", separated from his second wife and their son, became Michelle Ann Duff and moved to live in downtown Toronto. She completed her sex transition in 1987 and, 12 years later, published her autobiography entitled *Make Haste Slowly*.

❧ PEDROSA "THE PATIENT" ❧

Spanish racer Daniel Pedrosa's only nickname is Dani, but if Valentino Rossi is *"Il Dottore"* (the Doctor), then Dani might be *"El Paciente"* (the Patient). This was his list of broken bones between 2003 and 2013:

Year	Injury	Year	Injury
2003	broken ankles	2009	broken arm
2005	broken arm	2009	broken femur
2006	broken toe	2010	broken collarbone
2008	broken fingers	2011	broken collarbone
2008	broken wrist	2013	broken collarbone

Did You Know That?

Dani Pedrosa is a three-times World Champion, winning the 125cc title in 2003 and 250cc crown in both 2004 and 2005. As of the end of the 2015 season, in all classes, Pedrosa had won 51 races in 244 starts, including at least one in each of his ten seasons in MotoGP.

❧ MAN UP ❧

In June 1949, Manliefe Barrington, from Monkstown, County Dublin, Republic of Ireland, won the inaugural 250cc event in the F.I.M. World Championship. The race was part of the Isle of Man TT series.

❧ THE SWISS GRAND PRIX ❧

The Swiss Grand Prix formed part of the F.I.M. World Championship calendar for only the first six years, 1949–54, and British racers won all of them. Leslie Graham won the inaugural race for AJS at the 4.524-mile (7.28km) Circuit Bremgarten in Bern, and went on to become the 500cc World Champion. The Swiss Grand Prix moved to a street circuit in Geneva in 1950, but the result was the same, Graham (AJS), taking the chequered flag. The last four Swiss GPs were back at the Circuit Bremgarten, and the winners were Fergus Anderson (1951, Moto Guzzi), Jack Brett (1952, AJS) and Geoff Duke (1953 and 1954, both times on a Gilera). In the wake of the 1955 Le Mans 24 Hours disaster, when 83 spectators and driver Pierre Levegh perished, the Swiss Government banned spectator racing sports, except for hill-climbing and rallying. In June 2007, the lower house of the Swiss parliament voted, 97 to 77, to lift the ban, but the upper house overruled them three times, and the proposal was withdrawn in 2009.

● 1964 500CC FINAL STANDINGS (TOP 10) ●

Pos	Rider	Nationality	Bike	Pts
1.	Mike Hailwood	(GBR)	MV Agusta	40
2.	Jack Ahearn	(AUS)	Norton	25
=	Phil Read	(GBR)	Matchless/Norton	25
4.	Mike Duff	(CAN)	Norton/Matchless	18
5.	Paddy Driver	(RSA)	Matchless	16
6.	Fred Stevens	(GBR)	Matchless/Norton	8
7.	Gyula Marsovszky	(SUI)	Matchless	7
8.	Remo Venturi	(ITA)	Bianchi	6
=	Benedicto Caldarella	(ARG)	Gilera	6
=	Derek Minter	(GBR)	Norton	6
=	Dick Creith	(NIR)	Norton	6

● CONSTRUCTORS' FINAL STANDINGS (TOP 5) ●

Pos	Team	Nationality	Pts
1.	MV Agusta	(ITA)	56
2.	Norton	(GBR)	43
3.	Matchless	(GBR)	40
4.	Bianchi	(ITA)	6
=	Gilera	(ITA)	6
=	CKEB	(URS)	6

● HOME WINS ●

Home wins are always special to all motorsports competitors and fans. Some are still waiting for that very special moment, such as Formula 1 Japanese fans; British motorcycle fans had their moment on day 1 when Harold Daniell (Norton) won the first ever 500cc Grand Prix, at the Isle of Man TT (officially the British GP) in 1949, and Freddie Frith (Velocette) claimed the 350cc event. The last two events in 1949 were the Ulster Grand Prix in Belfast and the Nations GP at Monza, Italy. At both meetings, all three races were won by home riders: Leslie Graham (riding an AJS in the 500cc), Freddie Frith (350cc) and Maurice Cann (Moto Guzzi, 250cc) winning in Northern Ireland, while Nello Pagani (Gilera, 500cc), Dario Ambrosini (Benelli, 250cc) and Gianni Leoni (Mondial, 125cc) triumphed at the long-time home of the Italian F1 GP. Graham won the 500cc World Championship, Frith the 350cc title and Pagani (Mondial) the 125cc crown. A second Italian, Bruno Ruffo (Moto Guzzi) won the 250cc World Championship.

⚙ GREATEST RACES (3) – 2007 CATALUNYA GP ⚙

The biggest thrill for many MotoGP fans is watching overtaking manoeuvres. The 2007 season had seen a change in the MotoGP class, with riders now permitted to race 800cc machines, making the bikes faster and the action even more spectacular.

And at the Catalunya Grand Prix, 110,000 spectators were treated to a ding-dong battle between Casey Stoner (Ducati) and five-time World Champion, Valentino Rossi (Yamaha). They had shared five of the six races to date, Stoner winning three times, Rossi twice.

Rossi started from pole, with Stoner fourth on the grid and, for most of the 25 laps, they swapped positions at the front. The Italian was smoother around the corners, but the Aussie held sway on the straights. Stoner may have been in only his second season in MotoGP, but he and his Ducati were a perfect match.

The contest went all the way to the chequered flag, where Stoner took a 0.069-second victory. Rossi was second with Spanish hero Dani Pedrosa less than half a second behind in third. This success launched Stoner on a storming run to the World Championship, winning six of the last 11 races.

2007 Catalunya Grand Prix – Circuit de Catalunya – Sunday 10 June

Pos	Pts	Rider (Nationality)	Bike	Time/Gap
1.	25	Casey Stoner (AUS)	Ducati	43m 16.907s
2.	20	Valentino Rossi (ITA)	Yamaha	+0.069s
3.	16	Dani Pedrosa (SPA)	Honda	+0.390s
4.	13	John Hopkins (USA)	Suzuki	+7.814s
5.	11	Randy de Puniet (FRA)	Kawasaki	+17.853s

Did You Know That?
This was the ninth consecutive MotoGP race which the pole-sitter had failed to win. Valentino Rossi was fastest in qualifying for seven of these – and won the other two!

⚙ TWO NEW COUNTRIES JOIN THE PARTY ⚙

Two new Grands Prix were added to the calendar, for the 1951 Motorcycle World Championship, in Spain and France. The inaugural Spanish Grand Prix, at the Montjuic Circuit, Barcelona, replaced the Isle of Man TT as the season-opener and the first 500cc winner was Umberto Masetti riding for Gilera. The sixth race of 1951 was at Circuit d'Albi, Le Sequestre, France. The winner, Gilera's Alfredo Milani, enjoyed his first ever 500cc World Championship success.

● 1965 500CC FINAL STANDINGS (TOP 10) ●

Pos	Rider	Nationality	Bike	Pts
1.	Mike Hailwood	(GBR)	MV Agusta	48
2.	Giacomo Agostini	(ITA)	MV Agusta	38
3.	Paddy Driver	(RSA)	Matchless	26
4.	Fred Stevens	(GBR)	Matchless	15
5.	Jack Ahearn	(AUS)	Norton	9
6.	Dick Creith	(NIR)	Norton	8
=	Jack Findlay	(AUS)	Matchless	8
8.	Joe Dunphy	(GBR)	Norton	6
=	Buddy Parriott	(USA)	Norton	6
10.	Frantisek Stastny	(TCH)	Jawa	5

● CONSTRUCTORS' FINAL STANDINGS (TOP 5) ●

Pos	Team	Nationality	Pts
1.	MV Agusta	(ITA)	72
2.	Norton	(GBR)	38
3.	Matchless	(GBR)	36
4.	JAWA	(CZE)	5
5.	Moto Guzzi	(ITA)	2

● ULSTER'S HERO ●

Local boy, Cromie McCandless, who was born in Hillsborough, County Down, Northern Ireland, won the 1952 500cc Ulster Grand Prix riding a Norton/Gilera, thereby becoming the first Ulsterman to win his home race in the senior division. It was his only 500cc victory although he did win the Ultra Lightweight class in the 1951 Isle of Man TT. It was not McCandless's only victory in his home GP, but he got no World Championship points for winning the 1951 125cc race. The F.I.M. ruled that as there were only four competitors at the start of the race, the result would not count in the final standings.

● BRETT'S DAY IN THE SUN ●

Although his motorcycle racing career lasted from 1949–60, Jack Brett's victory in the 1952 500cc Swiss Grand Prix was his only one in the premier class. However, Brett did win the 500cc North West 200 race in Northern Ireland twice, 1957 and 1958. Brett was aged 40 when he finished fifth in the 1947 500cc World Championship.

⚜ THE BELLS STOPPED RINGING IN URBINA ⚜

Whenever Valentino Rossi won a Motorcycle Grand Prix, the church bells in his home town of Urbino in the Tavullia region of Italy rang out in celebration. The bells first tolled in his debut season in the 125cc World Championship when he won the Czech Republic Grand Prix at Brno on 18 August 1996 for Aprilia. They would toll a further 104 times – racing for Aprilia, Honda and Yamaha – up to the end of the 2010 season but, over the course of the next two years, a hush fell over Urbino because the bells stopped ringing. Rossi had left Yamaha after winning four MotoGP World Championships in seven seasons, to join Italian manufacturer Ducati, creating a firestorm of excitement across the sport. Sadly the Italian "marriage made in heaven" turned into a nightmare as Rossi was rarely even competitive; in 2011 he finished seventh in the World Championship – his lowest position since his maiden season in 125cc – and had a best result of third in the French Grand Prix. There was an improvement in 2012, but it was minimal: sixth in the World Championship and two second places (in the French and San Marino GPs) and his adoring fans were delighted when it was announced that Rossi would be returning to Yamaha for the 2013 season. The bells have started tolling again, on 29 June 2013, when Rossi won the Dutch TT, since when he won twice in 2014 and four times in 2015.

⚜ MOST CONSECUTIVE GP STARTS ⚜

Up to the end of the 2015 season, these are the top five riders in terms of consecutive GP starts in any of MotoGP, Moto2 and Moto3. Some of these racers, such as Andrea Dovizioso and Valentino Rossi, have progressed through the ranks without missing a race.

Rank	Rider (Nationality)	Starts
1.	Andrea Dovizioso (ITA)	238
2.	Valentino Rossi (ITA)	230
3.	Max Biaggi (ITA)	201
4.	Randy de Puniet (FRA)	190
5.	Sandro Cortese (GER)	186

Did You Know That?
Alessandro "Sandro" Cortese was born in Ochsenhausen, Germany, on 6 January 1990, the son of an Italian father and German mother. He began his racing career aged just nine, on pocket bikes (miniature motorcycles) and was European Pocket Bike and German Mini Bike champion. In 2012, he took the Moto3 crown for KTM.

● CONSTRUCTORS' WORLD CHAMPIONSHIP ●

Only eight manufacturers from three countries, Great Britain, Italy and Japan, have won the Constructors' World Championship (in 500cc/MotoGP) since the inaugural competition in 1949. This is the full list:

1949	AJS	GBR	1983	Honda	JPN
1950	Norton	GBR	1984	Honda	JPN
1951	Norton	GBR	1985	Honda	JPN
1952	Gilera	ITA	1986	Yamaha	JPN
1953	Gilera	ITA	1987	Yamaha	JPN
1954*	Gilera	ITA	1988	Yamaha	JPN
1955	Gilera	ITA	1989	Honda	JPN
1956	MV Agusta	ITA	1990	Yamaha	JPN
1957	Gilera	ITA	1991	Yamaha	JPN
1958	MV Agusta	ITA	1992	Honda	JPN
1959	MV Agusta	ITA	1993	Yamaha	JPN
1960	MV Agusta	ITA	1994	Honda	JPN
1961	MV Agusta	ITA	1995	Honda	JPN
1962	MV Agusta	ITA	1996	Honda	JPN
1963	MV Agusta	ITA	1997	Honda	JPN
1964	MV Agusta	ITA	1998	Honda	JPN
1965	MV Agusta	ITA	1999	Honda	JPN
1966	Honda	JPN	2000	Yamaha	JPN
1967	MV Agusta	ITA	2001	Honda	JPN
1968	MV Agusta	ITA	2002	Honda	JPN
1969	MV Agusta	ITA	2003	Honda	JPN
1970	MV Agusta	ITA	2004	Honda	JPN
1971	MV Agusta	ITA	2005	Yamaha	JPN
1972	MV Agusta	ITA	2006	Honda	JPN
1973	MV Agusta	ITA	2007	Ducati	ITA
1974	Yamaha	JPN	2008	Yamaha	JPN
1975	Yamaha	JPN	2009	Yamaha	JPN
1976	Suzuki	JPN	2010	Yamaha	JPN
1977	Suzuki	JPN	2011	Honda	JPN
1978	Suzuki	JPN	2012	Honda	JPN
1979	Suzuki	JPN	2013	Honda	JPN
1980	Suzuki	JPN	2014	Honda	JPN
1981	Suzuki	JPN	2015	Yamaha	JPN
1982	Suzuki	JPN			

* The 1954 Constructors' Championship title was not recognized by the sport's governing body, the F.I.M., as a result of a dispute with manufacturers over the number of races in the season and the abolition of the riders' championship.

❂ WANNABES ❂

On the day Valentino Rossi won his first ever Motorcycle Grand Prix race, the 125cc Czech Republic GP at Brno – 18 August 1996 – the Spice Girls' "Wannabe" was at No. 1 in the UK Singles Chart. By coincidence, as of 2015, Rossi has been a World Champion, in all classes, nine times and the Spice Girls were at No. 1 nine times.

❂ TYRED OUT ❂

The 2015 Valencia Grand Prix was the last Grand Prix for Japanese tyre company Bridgestone as the sole tyre supplier in MotoGP. From 2016, all of the machines will run on rubber provided by Michelin. For most of the F.I.M. World Championship's history riders, or more usually teams, could choose which tyres to use. However, no team used Dunlop after 2007 and Michelin decided to pull out after the 2008 season, so Bridgestone became the sole provider.

❂ KINGS OF YAMAHA ❂

Up to the end of the 2015 MotoGP season, Yamaha bikes had won more than 230 F.I.M. World Championship races, in either the 500cc class or its successor MotoGP. The manufacturer's two most successful riders formed the team in both 2014 and 2015, Valentino Rossi and Jorge Lorenzo. Of Rossi's 86 500cc/MotoGP wins, 53 were achieved riding a Yamaha (he was World Champion for them in 2004, 2005, 2008 and 2009), and the other 33 were sitting on a Honda. Lorenzo, the MotoGP World Champion in 2010, 2012 and 2015 – all for Yamaha – has won 40 times for the Japanese giants, although their MotoGP factory is based in Italy. Back in the days of the 500cc World Championship, "Steady" Eddie Lawson won 26 races for Yamaha, Wayne Rainey 24, and "King" Kenny Roberts enjoyed 22 race victories aboard a Yamaha.

Did You Know That?
Between them, Rossi and Lorenzo own more than 40 per cent of all Yamaha's 500cc/MotoGP race wins.

❂ TOP TEXAN ❂

Kevin Schwantz was born in Houston, Texas, on 19 June 1964. After learning the ropes in North America, he came over to ride in the 500cc World Championship in 1986. He won 25 GPs – second amongst all American racers – and was the 1993 500cc World Champion.

❂ PHIL READ MBE – THE PRINCE OF SPEED ❂

A household name in the 1960s and 1970s, whilst racing fearlessly on 125cc, 250cc, 350cc and 500cc bikes, Phillip William Read was born on 1 January 1939 in Luton, England. Nicknamed "The Prince of Speed", he was the first man to win World Championships at 125cc, 250cc and 500cc.

Phil's interest in bikes began at an early age and he got his first bike, a Velocette KSS, in 1955 before acquiring a BSA Gold Star DBD32. In 1958, aged 19 and an apprentice fitter at a local industrial machinery company, he started competing in amateur short-circuit racing. Two years later, Phil won the Junior Manx Grand Prix and broke the existing speed record, and in 1961, he won the Junior (350cc) TT race on another Norton. Phil also won the 1962 and 1963 Thruxton 500 endurance races. He stepped up to Grand Prix road racing in 1963 when he replaced the injured Derek Minter at the Scuderia Duke Gilera team and made an immediate impact. Phil's 500cc debut came in the Isle of Man TT, and he made a spectacular impression, finishing third, and he followed that up with podium places in both of his next two races, the Dutch TT at Assen and the Belgian GP at Spa-Francorchamps.

Yamaha offered Phil £5,000 to ride for them in 1964. He accepted and gave the Japanese giant their first World Championship, winning five of 11 250cc races in the 1964 season. Phil retained the 250cc World Championship for Yamaha, this time winning seven of 13 GPs. Over the next two seasons Phil had to cede the title to another Brit, Mike Hailwood on a Honda – the latter year only on wins countback. Also in 1967, Phil was second in the 125cc World Championship, beaten by another British (and Yamaha) racer, Bill Ivy. Yamaha set their sights on winning the 125cc World Championship with Read and the 250cc World Championship with Ivy. Phil, however, defied team orders and not only won the 125cc World Championship but also beat Ivy in the 250cc class, albeit on a tie-break of elapsed time. The manufacturer was furious and sacked him, leaving him without a works ride in 1969 or 1970.

Phil was back in 1971, and claimed the 250cc World Championship on a private Yamaha-powered Eric Cheney-designed chassis, Yamaha having withdrawn from GP racing in 1970. It was his fifth World Championship crown and he became the first World Champion as a privateer. MV Agusta signed him in 1972 and the following year he clinched the 500cc World Championship – he also finished third in the 350cc class. Phil made it back-to-back 500cc World Championships in 1974 to give the legendary Italian marque what turned out to be their last ever world title.

In 1975, Phil and MV Agusta were no match for Giacomo Agostini and Yamaha, though Read did finish second in the 500cc World Championship. That year's season-ending 500cc Czechoslovakian Grand Prix proved to be his 52nd and last Grand Prix victory. Phil switched to a privateer Suzuki, without any success in 1969, and, at the end of the season, he retired. In 1979, he was awarded the MBE and, in 2002, the F.I.M. – motorcycling racing's governing body – named Phil a Grand Prix "Legend".

Did You Know That?
Phil's 1974 500cc World Championship was the last time a four-stroke motorcycle won a world title until the advent of the MotoGP class in 2002.

❂ 1966 500CC FINAL STANDINGS (TOP 10) ❂

Pos	Rider	Nationality	Bike	Pts
1.	Giacomo Agostini	(ITA)	MV Agusta	36
2.	Mike Hailwood	(GBR)	Honda	30
3.	Jack Findlay	(AUS)	Matchless	20
4.	Frantisek Stastny	(TCH)	Jawa-CZ	17
5.	Jim Redman	(RHO)	Honda	16
6.	Gyula Marsovszky	(SUI)	Matchless	13
7.	Jack Ahearn	(AUS)	Norton	13
8.	Stuart Graham	(GBR)	Matchless	11
9.	Peter Williams	(GBR)	Matchless/AJS	7
10.	Chris Conn	(GBR)	Norton	6
=	Ron Chandler	(GBR)	Matchless	6

❂ CONSTRUCTORS' FINAL STANDINGS (TOP 5) ❂

Pos	Team	Nationality	Pts
1.	MV Agusta	(ITA)	54
2.	Honda	(JPN)	46
3.	Matchless	(GBR)	38
4.	Norton	(GBR)	24
5.	Jawa-CZ	(CZE)	17

❂ FAST TALK (5) ❂

"Why would you make a motorcycle that you can't wheelie?"
Kenny Roberts

⚫ 1967 500CC FINAL STANDINGS (TOP 10) ⚫

Pos	Rider	Nationality	Bike	Pts
1.	Giacomo Agostini	(ITA)	MV Agusta	46
=	Mike Hailwood	(GBR)	Honda	46
3.	John Hartle	(GBR)	Matchless/Kirby-Metisse	22
4.	Peter Williams	(GBR)	Matchless	16
5.	Jack Findlay	(AUS)	Matchless/Norton	15
6.	Fred Stevens	(GBR)	Hannah-Paton	11
7.	John Cooper	(GBR)	Norton	8
8.	Gyula Marsovszky	(SUI)	Matchless	7
9.	Billie Nelson	(GBR)	Norton	6
=	Steve Spencer	(GBR)	Norton	6

⚫ CONSTRUCTORS' FINAL STANDINGS (TOP 5) ⚫

Pos	Team	Nationality	Pts
1.	MV Agusta	(ITA)	58
2.	Honda	(JPN)	52
3.	Matchless	(GBR)	34
4.	Norton	(GBR)	25
5.	Metisse	(GBR)	22

⚫ HAYDEN BOWS OUT ⚫

Nicky Hayden, born 30 July 1981, in Kentucky, USA, was the 2006 MotoGP World Champion, and rode in his last race in the 2015 Valencia Grand Prix before moving to compete in the Superbike World Championship. The F.I.M., the sport's governing body, recognized Hayden's achievements by naming him MotoGP's 22nd "Legend".

⚫ SUPER CAL ⚫

Englishman Cal Crutchlow – he was born in Coventry on 29 October 1985 – has ridden in MotoGP since 2011, and enjoyed eight podium finishes though he has yet to win a race. His consistency has, however, been rewarded with five top-10 places in the MotoGP World Championship, with a best of fifth overall in 2013. Before he joined MotoGP, Cal rode in Supersport and Superbikes. In 2009 he won the Supersport World Championship and, a year later, claimed five race victories in the World Superbike Championship on his way to fifth in the final table.

❀ FEAST OR FAMINE FOR SCHWANTZ ❀

Kevin Schwantz won twice in the first six races of the 1988 season, the Japan and West Germany Grands Prix. In the last eight races, however, he managed only two more podium finishes, third places in both France and Brazil. Wayne Rainey collected only one victory in the season, the British GP, but he was second twice and fourth four times. It meant that Rainey collected 189 points in the 500cc World Championship, good enough for third overall, behind Eddie Lawson and Wayne Gardner. Schwantz, however, managed only 119 points and was eighth in the final standings.

❀ LEADING THE WAY FOR SPAIN ❀

In the 21st century, racers from Spain and Italy have led the way in terms of 500cc/MotoGP World Championship victories. Italian World Champions date back to the 1950s; Spain's first winner came as recently as 1999. The man who broke the Spanish duck was also the first racer from the country to win a race in the class, Alex Criville. Born on 4 March 1970, in Barcelona, Criville's desire to race was so great, he falsified his birthdate to get a licence before his 15th birthday – the minimum age limit in Spain. His World Championship debut came aged 17 at Jerez, in the 1987 80cc Spanish Grand Prix. Two years later, he won his first Grand Prix, the 125cc Australian GP, and went on to become the 125cc World Champion. In 1992, Alex was racing in the 500cc class, riding a Honda, and won his first race at Assen in the Dutch TT. Mick Doohan's career-ending injury gave Alex the chance to be the Honda No.1 rider in 1999 and he took it with both hands, winning six races and becoming World Champion. He won only one more race before leaving the World Championship after the 2001 season.

Did You Know That?
Prior to his 1999 500cc World Championship season, Alex had won only eight times in 55 starts. However, he was runner-up, behind Honda team-mate Mick Doohan, in the 1996 World Championship.

❀ THAT'S A LOT OF LAPS ❀

At the end of the 2012 MotoGP season, it was estimated that nine-time World Champion Valentino Rossi had ridden approximately 77,000 miles in his Grand Prix career, the equivalent of circumnavigating planet Earth more than three times.

◉ 1968 500CC FINAL STANDINGS (TOP 10) ◉

Pos	Rider	Nationality	Bike	Pts
1.	Giacomo Agostini	(ITA)	MV Agusta	48
2.	Jack Findlay	(AUS)	Matchless/Cardani	30
=	Gyula Marsovszky	(SUI)	Matchless/Seeley-Matchless	30
4.	Alberto Pagani	(ITA)	Linto	10
5.	Robin Fitton	(GBR)	Norton	9
6.	Peter Williams	(GBR)	Arter-Matchless	9
7.	Derek Woodman	(GBR)	Seeley	8
8.	John Cooper	(GBR)	Seeley/Norton	8
9.	Dan Shorey	(GBR)	Norton	7
10.	Angelo Bergamonti	(ITA)	Paton	7
=	Kel Carruthers	(AUS)	Norton/Westlake	7

◉ CONSTRUCTORS' FINAL STANDINGS (TOP 5) ◉

Pos	Team	Nationality	Pts
1.	MV Agusta	(ITA)	80
2.	Matchless	(GBR)	45
3.	Norton	(GBR)	30
4.	Seeley	(GBR)	21
5.	Paton	(ITA)	12

◉ A HOLE IN DANI'S CV ◉

Dani Pedrosa has enjoyed a successful career in MotoGP, claiming 100 podium finishes in motorcycle racing's elite class. He was 125cc World Champion in 2003 and 250cc World Champion in both 2004 and 2005. Despite taking pole position on 28 occasions and setting the fastest laps in races 41 times, there is one gaping hole in Dani's career. No racer has won more than his 28 500cc/MotoGP races and not been World Champion. In 10 World Championship seasons, Dani has finished second, third and fourth three times each and fifth once.

◉ THIRD PLACE NOT IN THEIR VOCABULARIES ◉

Between them Giacomo Agostini and John Surtees won a dozen 500cc World Championships and when it came to winning races, they were on the top step of the podium 90 times. However, although they achieved 22 runners-up positions, neither Agostini nor Surtees ever finished third in a 500cc World Championship race.

❂ POINTS SCORING SYSTEM ❂

The F.I.M. Motorcycle World Championship had a bewildering 18 different scoring systems in its first 43 seasons. Most of the changes, however, revolved around the number of scores which counted. Since 1977, all races have scored in the final standings, and there have been no changes since 1993. These have been the scoring systems:

Year/s	Places	1	2	3	4	5	6	7	8	9	10	11	12	13	14	15
1949	1–5	10	8	7	6	5										
1950–68	1–6	8	6	4	3	2	1									
1969–87	1–10	15	12	10	8	6	5	4	3	2	1					
1988–91	1–15	20	17	15	13	11	10	9	8	7	6	5	4	3	2	1
1992	1–10	20	15	12	10	8	6	4	3	2	1					
1993–	1–15	25	20	16	13	11	10	9	8	7	6	5	4	3	2	1

In many years of the World Championship, racers collected maximum points by winning the required number of races, but there was no season when two achieved the maximum score. These were the number of best results required in each season:

Year/s	Best results
1949	3
1950	4
1951–55	5
1956–60	4
1961	6
1962–64	5
1965	6
1966	5
1967–68	6
1969	7
1970–71	6
1972	7
1973–75	6
1976	6*

* *Unlike in previous years, when the best scores from the whole season counted, in 1976, the best three scores from the first five races and the best three scores from the last five races would count.*

Did You Know That?
Between 1949 and 1975, there was one extra point awarded to the rider who set the fastest lap, but they had to finish the race.

🏁 1969 500CC FINAL STANDINGS (TOP 10) 🏁

Pos	Rider	Nationality	Bike	Pts
1.	Giacomo Agostini	(ITA)	MV Agusta	105
2.	Gyula Marsovszky	(SUI)	Librenti/Linto	47
3.	Godfrey Nash	(GBR)	Norton	45
4.	Billie Nelson	(GBR)	Paton	42
5.	Alan Barnett	(GBR)	Kirby-Metisse	32
6.	Steve Ellis	(GBR)	Linto	26
7.	Ron Chandler	(GBR)	Seeley-Matchless	25
8.	Gilberto Milani	(ITA)	Aermacchi	24
9.	Robin Fitton	(GBR)	Norton	19
10.	Brian Steenson	(NIR)	Seeley-Matchless	18
=	John Dodds	(AUS)	Linto/Seeley-Matchless	18
=	Terry Dennehy	(AUS)	Linto/Seeley-URS	18

🏁 CONSTRUCTORS' FINAL STANDINGS (TOP 5) 🏁

Pos	Team	Nationality	Pts
1.	MV Agusta	(ITA)	150
2.	Linto	(ITA)	86
3.	Matchless	(GBR)	78
4.	Seeley	(GBR)	77
5.	Paton	(ITA)	70

🏁 BUSMAN'S HOLIDAY 🏁

Troy Bayliss, born 30 March 1969 in New South Wales, Australia, won three World Superbikes titles before riding for Ducati in the 2003 MotoGP World Championship, (he had ridden in the 1997 250cc Australian Grand Prix, finishing sixth). He made an immediate impact, finishing third in the 2003 Spanish, German and Czech Republic Grands Prix and his 128 points gave him sixth place in the MotoGP World Championship table. Troy had a frustrating 2004 season, retiring eight times in the 16 races, and Ducati ended his contract. At Honda in 2005, a broken arm ended Troy's season and he returned to Superbikes, immediately winning the title. Ducati offered him a ride in the season-ending 2006 Valencia GP, and Troy showed his true colours. He qualified second and led almost all the way before taking his only chequered flag in MotoGP.

Did You Know That?
Troy drove in three V8 Supercars races in 2009 but did not score a point.

● FANTASY 500CC/MOTOGP
SPANISH STARTING GRID ●

(to the end of the 2015 season)

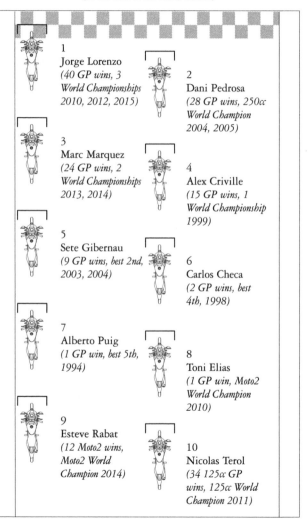

1
Jorge Lorenzo
(40 GP wins, 3
World Championships
2010, 2012, 2015)

2
Dani Pedrosa
(28 GP wins, 250cc
World Champion
2004, 2005)

3
Marc Marquez
(24 GP wins, 2
World Championships
2013, 2014)

4
Alex Criville
(15 GP wins, 1
World Championship
1999)

5
Sete Gibernau
(9 GP wins, best 2nd,
2003, 2004)

6
Carlos Checa
(2 GP wins, best
4th, 1998)

7
Alberto Puig
(1 GP win, best 5th,
1994)

8
Toni Elias
(1 GP win, Moto2
World Champion
2010)

9
Esteve Rabat
(12 Moto2 wins,
Moto2 World
Champion 2014)

10
Nicolas Terol
(34 125cc GP
wins, 125cc World
Champion 2011)

● 1970 500CC FINAL STANDINGS (TOP 10) ●

Pos	Rider	Nationality	Bike	Pts
1.	Giacomo Agostini	(ITA)	MV Agusta	90
2.	Ginger Molloy	(NZL)	Bultaco/Kawasaki	62
3.	Angelo Bergamonti	(ITA)	Aermacchi/MV Agusta	59
4.	Tommy Robb	(NIR)	Seeley	36
5.	Alberto Pagani	(ITA)	Linto	30
6.	Alan Barnett	(GBR)	Seeley-Matchless	24
=	Christian Ravel	(FRA)	Kawasaki	24
=	Jack Findlay	(AUS)	Seeley-Matchless/ Seeley-Suzuki	24
=	Martti Pesonen	(FIN)	Yamaha	24
10.	Peter Williams	(GBR)	Matchless	22

● CONSTRUCTORS' FINAL STANDINGS (TOP 5) ●

Pos	Team	Nationality	Pts
1.	MV Agusta	(ITA)	165
2.	Kawasaki	(JPN)	106
3.	Seeley	(GBR)	82
4.	Aermacchi	(ITA)	47
5.	Linto	(ITA)	42

● ALMOST COMPLETE FUTILITY ●

In the 11-race 1961 500cc World Championship, no fewer than 62 men appeared in a single event but failed to finish. Twenty other riders contested more than one event and did not complete any of them. In addition, 31 racers managed to get round, but did not register a single 500cc World Championship point (tenth place brought one point, the winner earned 15). Amazingly there were still 52 men who did collect at least one point, meaning a total of 165 people contested at least a single race in the season. New Zealander Keith Turner was the only person to start all 11 races, but he retired three times on his way to finishing runner-up behind World Champion Giacomo Agostini, winner of the first eight GPs.

● SHORTER CIRCUIT ●

The Isle of Man TT for motorbikes with engine capacity up to 350cc was staged on the 10.92-mile Clypse Course from 1954 to 1959. After that, races were on the 37.73-mile Snaefell Mountain Course.

⦿ GREATEST RACES (4) – 2005 SPANISH GP ⦿

The Spanish Grand Prix at Jerez has produced some exhilarating races over the years and the odd spat or two. The 2005 edition produced a spikey affair on the track and the odd word or two in *parc ferme* after the race.

It was the opening race of the 2005 season and it all came down to the last corner on the final lap. Home favourite, Sete Giberneau (Honda), and Valentino Rossi (Yamaha) – going for a fifth successive World Championship – had swapped the race lead several times. Giberneau led into the last corner but Rossi, always looking for the tiniest gap, nipped up his inside, forcing the Honda into the gravel. Rossi took the chequered flag 8.631 seconds in front of a disgusted Giberneau.

Words were exchanged in *parc ferme*. At the post-race press conference, the Italian admitted that it had been a "hard overtake" and he understood the Spaniard's anger, but this was racing. Gibernau, who had finished runner-up to Rossi in the 2003 and 2004 World Championships when he was a Telefonica Movistar Honda rider, just glared at Rossi.

2005 Spanish Grand Prix – Circuito de Jerez – Sunday 10 April

Pos	Pts	Rider (Nationality)	Bike	Time/Gap
1.	25	Valentino Rossi (ITA)	Yamaha	45m 43.156s
2.	20	Sete Gibernau (SPA)	Honda	+8.631s
3.	16	Marco Melandri (ITA)	Honda	+18.460s
4.	13	Alex Barros (BRA)	Honda	+26.938s
5.	11	Shinya Nakano (JAP)	Kawasaki	+27.659s

Did You Know That?
Sete Gibernau is the grandson of Francisco Xavier "Paco" Bulto, the founder of Bultaco, the Spanish motorcycle manufacturer.

⦿ GOOD DAYS AND BAD FOR PAGANI ⦿

Italian racer Alberto Pagani rode for Linto in the 1970 500cc World Championship and managed to finish fifth overall. He rode in eight races and enjoyed podium finishes three times – admittedly always on the bottom step – in the French Grand Prix, the Dutch TT and the Finnish GP. Unfortunately, in all of the other five races, he failed to finish. That said, winning wasn't really on the agenda as Pagani's compatriot Giacomo Agostini took care of first place in rounds 1–10 inclusive and didn't contest the season-ending Grand Prix in Spain.

● 1971 500CC FINAL STANDINGS (TOP 10) ●

Pos	Rider	Nationality	Bike	Pts
1.	Giacomo Agostini	(ITA)	MV Agusta	90
2.	Keith Turner	(NZL)	Coleman-Suzuki	58
3.	Rob Bron	(NED)	Suzuki	57
4.	Dave Simmonds	(GBR)	Kawasaki	52
5.	Jack Findlay	(AUS)	Suzuki/Jada	50
6.	Eric Offenstadt	(FRA)	Kawasaki	32
7.	Tommy Robb	(NIR)	Hurst-Seeley/Matchless	31
8.	Alberto Pagani	(ITA)	Linto/MV Agusta	29
9.	Kaarlo Koivuniemi	(FIN)	Seeley-Matchless	24
10.	Ron Chandler	(GBR)	Kawasaki	19

● CONSTRUCTORS' FINAL STANDINGS (TOP 5) ●

Pos	Team	Nationality	Pts
1.	MV Agusta	(ITA)	135
2.	Suzuku	(JPN)	107
3.	Kawasaki	(JPN)	105
4.	Seeley	(GBR)	58
5.	Yamaha	(JPN)	33

● BIKES IN HIS OR HER BLOOD ●

Michael Duff's motorcycle career was nothing if not varied. He was reasonably successful as a racer between 1960 and 1967 – winning the 1965 250cc Finnish Grand Prix and coming second in the 250cc World Championship standings that year. In 1967, he separated from his first wife, who was Finnish (they had two children together), moved from Canada to California and became the associate editor of *Cycle World* magazine. Mike's love of racing was too strong, and he was back on a bike, winning the Eastern Canadian Championship in 1969. In 1970, he started a Yamaha dealership, which he ran until 1978, when he remarried and had another son. His next job was as a specialized motorcycle mechanic in the Greater Toronto area. In 1984, he left his wife and underwent gender reassignment.

● A LONG WAIT ●

Tommy Robb's last race in the Motorcycle World Championship was the 1973 125cc Isle of Man TT. He went out a winner, ending a run of 58 races and 11 years since he had won the 1962 350cc Finnish GP.

❂ HIGH NOON IN VALENCIA ❂

Going into the final round of the 2015 MotoGP World Championship season, the Valencia GP, on the streets of the Spanish city, only two riders had a chance to win the overall title, Yamaha team-mates, seven-times MotoGP champion Valentino Rossi and Jorge Lorenzo, twice a World Champion in the previous five years. The Italian held a six-point advantage, but an incident involving the two-time defending World Champion Marc Marquez in the penultimate round meant that Rossi would be forced to start from the back of the grid. The count-back of victories gave Lorenzo another advantage, so a victory for the Spaniard meant Rossi had to finish second, though if *Il Dottore* finished in front of his team-mate, he would join his legendary compatriot Giacomo Agostini with eight top-class World Championships.

Spanish riders filled the first four places on the grid, with Lorenzo on pole, Marquez second, Dani Pedrosa third and Aleix Espargaro fourth. If Rossi's fears that Lorenzo would get protection from his compatriots, irrespective of their employers – Marquez and Pedrosa were on Hondas, Espargaro on a Suzuki – then his task got even harder. However, Rossi does have the reputation of being one of the world's greatest ever riders of a motorcycle and he immediately set about overtaking his 23 rivals (Cal Crutchlow was forced to start from the pit-lane because of a mechanical issue). Seething at what he perceived as an injustice, Rossi rode magnificently and was up to eighth place after 10 laps.

Up ahead of him, the first four were Lorenzo, Marquez, Pedrosa and Italian Andrea Dovizioso, but the gap to Rossi was very big – more than 11 seconds. As the race moved into the closing stages, Rossi's only hope of winning the World Championship was for Lorenzo to go off the track, or crash, or suffer a major performance problem. Unbeknownst to the Italian, both Lorenzo and Marquez were having difficulties with their tyres and neither felt able to race absolutely flat out. The defending champion, however, was going slightly the better and, in most cases, might have been expected to attack the race leader, but he was content to hold on to second place. At the chequered flag, Lorenzo led Marquez by 0.263 of a second and Pedrosa by 0.654. Rossi crossed the line almost 20 seconds later in fourth place.

Did You Know That?
Despite starting from pit-lane Crutchlow rode a brilliant race to finish in ninth place.

⚜ GIACOMO AGOSTINI – IL MEGLIO ⚜

Italy's best (*Il Meglio*) motorcycle racer of all time is Giacomo Agostini, born on 16 June 1942 in Brescia. The eldest of four brothers, Giacomo's father did not approve of him racing motorcycles but once he realized his son was determined to make a career on two wheels he gave Giacomo his full support. In 1963, "Ago", as he is known, won the 175cc Italian Grand Prix on a Morini. The following year the Morini factory signed him as a works rider and their faith in the 21-year-old was rewarded when he won the 350cc Italian Grand Prix and finished fourth in both the German and Nations 250cc Grands Prix. Team owner Count Alfonso Morini knew he could not hold on to Giacomo and, in 1965, MV Agusta signed him. He made a sensational start to his MV Agusta career by winning the season-opening 350cc German Grand Prix, and finished as World Championship runner-up in both the 350cc class, behind Jim Redman, and the 500cc category, behind Mike Hailwood.

Giacomo became MV Augusta's No.1 racer when Hailwood joined for Honda for 1966. In a season-long battle for the 500cc World Championship, the former team-mates both won three Grands Prix, but Ago enjoyed five more podium finishes, compared to "Mike the Bike's" one, and claimed his first 500cc World Championship (the roles were reversed in the 350cc class). Over the next six years Giacomo was almost unbeatable in both classes, winning the 500cc World Championship every year 1967–72 and the 350cc title from 1968–72 inclusive. Between 1968 and 1971, Ago retired from three 350cc Grands Prix and one 500cc race; the other 31 350cc and 38 at 500cc ended with Giacomo on top of the podium. Then, in 1972, he won a record 11 times in 12 500cc starts.

Phil Read joined MV Agusta for the 1973 season and immediately won the 500cc World Championship, from Konig's Jim Newcombe, with Giacomo third. However the Italian did win his 13th world title in the 350cc class. Ago joined Yamaha for the 1974 season and finished a disappointing fourth in the 500cc World Championship, behind the MV Agusta duo of Read and Franco Bonera and, surprisingly, Yahama team-mate Finnish rookie Teuvo Lansivuori. In the 350cc World Championship, however, Giacomo remained peerless and won a seventh consecutive title.

Ago bounced back in 1975, and after a thrilling battle in the season-ending Czechoslovakian GP, at Brno, although Read won the race, Giacomo, runner-up, took the World Championship, his eighth (15th in all classes) but Yamaha's first. More significantly, it was not only the first 500cc World Championship for a two-stroke machine but also the first time since 1957 that the champion was not riding for MV Agusta.

Giacomo returned to MV Agusta for the 1976 season and won both the 350cc Dutch TT and the 500cc German GP, the last two of his career. The victory at the Nurburgring was his 68th in 500cc and the win at Assen was his 54th at 350cc.

Did You Know That?
In the opening round of the 2015 MotoGP World Championship, Valentino Rossi overtook Agostini's record of 69 fastest laps in the elite competition.

● 1972 500CC FINAL STANDINGS (TOP 10) ●

Pos	Rider	Nationality	Bike	Pts
1.	Giacomo Agostini	(ITA)	MV Agusta	105
2.	Alberto Pagani	(ITA)	MV Agusta	87
3.	Bruno Kneubuhler	(SUI)	Yamaha	54
4.	Rodney Gould	(GBR)	Yamaha	52
5.	Bo Granath	(SWE)	Husqvarna	47
6.	Chas Mortimer	(GBR)	Yamaha	42
=	Dave Simmonds	(GBR)	Kawasaki	42
8.	Billie Nelson	(GBR)	Honda/Yamaha/Paton	31
=	Jack Findlay	(AUS)	Jada-Suzuki	31
10.	Kim Newcombe	(NZL)	Konig	27

● CONSTRUCTORS' FINAL STANDINGS (TOP 5) ●

Pos	Team	Nationality	Pts
1.	MV Agusta	(ITA)	180
2.	Yamaha	(JPN)	124
3.	Kawasaki	(JPN)	75
4.	Jada-Suzuki	(JPN)	68
5.	Husqvarna	(SWE)	53

● LAST TIME ON THE ISLAND ●

The Isle of Man Tourist Trophy dates back to early in the 20th century and was the first event in the official F.I.M. World Championship. For the first 28 years of the World Championship it was effffectively the British Grand Prix but, after 1976, the British GP was held on the mainland, where it has remained ever since, either at Silverstone or Donington Park. The last winner of the IOM TT was an Irishman, Tom Herron, riding a Yamaha.

⚙ 1973 500CC FINAL STANDINGS (TOP 10) ⚙

Pos	Rider	Nationality	Bike	Pts
1.	Phil Read	(GBR)	MV Agusta	84
2.	Kim Newcombe	(NZL)	Konig	63
3.	Giacomo Agostini	(ITA)	MV Agusta	57
4.	Werner Giger	(SUI)	Yamaha	44
5.	Jack Findlay	(AUS)	Suzuki	38
6.	Bruno Kneubuhler	(SUI)	Yamaha	34
7.	Jarno Saarinen	(FIN)	Yamaha	30
8.	Hideo Kanaya	(JPN)	Yamaha	22
9.	Ernst Hiller	(FRG)	Konig	19
10.	Alex George	(GBR)	Yamaha	19

⚙ CONSTRUCTORS' FINAL STANDINGS (TOP 5) ⚙

Pos	Team	Nationality	Pts
1.	MV Agusta	(ITA)	117
2.	Yamaha	(JPN)	115
3.	Konig	(GER)	73
4.	Suzuku	(JPN)	65
5.	Kawasaki	(JPN)	28

⚙ FAST TALK (6) ⚙

"I'll get my mother to go to the shop and buy me a lot of new
underwear, because I think I'll need them."
*Jack Miller, 2014 Moto3 runner-up, after
agreeing to race in MotoGP in 2015*

⚙ FIRST WOMEN IN WORLD CHAMPIONSHIP ⚙

Beryl Swain, on an Itom, was the first woman to race solo in the
World Championship when she competed in the 1962 50cc race
at the Isle of Man TT, the first year the 50cc event carried World
Championship points. She finished 22nd in the race, but the male-
dominated F.I.M. immediately revoked her competitor's licence
by instituting a minimum weight limit for all competitors on the
grounds of safety. In the 1954 World Sidecar Championship, Inge
Stoll from Germany partnered Frenchman Jacques Drion and they
won two points after finishing fifth in the Isle of Man TT. Tragically,
both Stoll and Drion died on 24 August 1958 following a crash in
a non-World Championship event, the Czechoslovakian Grand Prix.

❀ MOTOGP LEGENDS ❀

The F.I.M.celebrates the careers of the greatest riders in motorcycle racing history by naming them Legends. In most cases, the riders have retired, but a few are awarded Legend status posthumously following fatal crashes on the track. The following 22 men have been honoured as Legends:

Rider	Nationality
Giacomo Agostini	ITA
Mick Doohan	AUS
Geoff Duke	GBR
Wayne Gardner	AUS
Nicky Hayden	USA
Mike Hailwood	GBR
Daijiro Kato	JAP
Eddie Lawson	USA
Anton Mang	GER
Angel Nieto	ESP
Wayne Rainey	USA
Phil Read	GBR
Jim Redman	RHO
Kenny Roberts Sr	USA
Jarno Saarinen	FIN
Kevin Schwantz	USA
Barry Sheene	GBR
Marco Simoncelli	ITA
Freddie Spencer	USA
Casey Stoner	AUS
John Surtees	GBR
Carlo Ubbiali	ITA

Did You Know That?
Just before his final race in MotoGP, the 2015 Valencia GP, the "Kentucky Kid" Nicky Hayden was announced as the 22nd Legend.

❀ NOT FOR LONG ❀

Venezuelan Johnny Cecotto was a World Championship star in the late 1970s and interest in his homeland resulted in the Venezuela Grand Prix, which was staged at San Carlos. It lasted only three years, 1977–79, and Barry Sheene won the 500cc race each time.

⚙ 1974 500CC FINAL STANDINGS (TOP 10) ⚙

Pos	Rider	Nationality	Bike	Pts
1.	Phil Read	(GBR)	MV Agusta	82
2.	Franco Bonera	(ITA)	MV Agusta	69
3.	Teuvo Lansivuori	(FIN)	Yamaha	67
4.	Giacomo Agostini	(ITA)	Yamaha	47
5.	Jack Findlay	(AUS)	Suzuki	34
6.	Barry Sheene	(GBR)	Suzuki	30
7.	Dieter Braun	(FRG)	Yamaha	22
=	Pentti Korhonen	(FIN)	Yamaha	22
9.	Billie Nelson	(GBR)	Yamaha	21
10.	Charlie Williams	(GBR)	Yamaha	18
=	John Williams	(GBR)	Yamaha	18

⚙ CONSTRUCTORS' FINAL STANDINGS (TOP 5) ⚙

Pos	Team	Nationality	Pts
1.	Yamaha	(JPN)	129
2.	MV Agusta	(ITA)	109
3.	Suzuki	(JPN)	52
4.	Harley Davidson	(ITA)	14
5.	Konig	(GER)	12

⚙ AROUND A VERY LONG TIME ⚙

Yamaha is the oldest manufacturer currently competing in MotoGP. The company was founded by Torakusu Yamaha on 12 October 1887, as the Nippon Gakki Company Limited, making pianos and reeds. Production of motorcycles did not start for almost 60 years, and the first bike bearing Yamaha's name came off the production line in Shizuoka in 1954, a 125cc bike, the YA-1, but nicknamed *Akatombo* (the red dragonfly). Today, Yamaha is a multi-national conglomerate, still producing musical instruments, and also boats, car engines, golf carts, industrial robots, RVs, swimming pools and even wheelchairs.

⚙ TALENT AND EXPERIENCE IN MOTO2 ⚙

The 2015 Moto2 grid included four previous 125cc or Moto3 World Champions: Sandro Cortese, Thomas Luthi, Alex Marquez and Julian Simon. The full-time entry list contained 14 previous Grand Prix winners, with a total of 83 GP victories between them.

⚘ WELSH ACE WINS FOR RHODESIA ⚘

Jim Redman was not the first World Champion – he won twice at 250cc and four times at 350cc – to ride under the flag of Rhodesia. That honour belongs to Welsh-born Gary Hocking, who remains the only man to win the 500cc World Championship representing Rhodesia, or its successor Zimbabwe. Hocking lost a close friend, Tom Phillis, at the 1962 Isle of Man TT and decided to switch to racing in Formula 1 cars. Tragically, he died even before his F1 career had begun, crashing fatally in practice for the 1962 Natal Grand Prix.

Did You Know That?
Gary Hocking won the 1961 World Championship in both the 350cc and 500cc classes.

⚘ ATMOSPHERE DISTURBER ⚘

George Brough was a motorbike racer and manufacturer from Nottingham, England. In 1924, the company produced the first bike which was able to clock 100mph. If the bike did not reach 100mph in testing, it was taken back to the shop and worked on until it did. Brough's machines, all custom built, were dubbed the "Rolls-Royce of Motorcycles" by *The Motor Cycle* newspaper's H. D. Teague, but Brough preferred to advertise his bikes as "Atmosphere Disturbers".

⚘ AUSTRIAN TRAGEDY LEADS TO PROTESTS ⚘

The death of Hans Stadelman in the 1977 350cc Austrian Grand Prix led to a sit-down protest by riders before the 125cc race could begin. In the 500cc class, World Champion to be Barry Sheene led an 18-man boycott of the GP, which was won by Britain's Jack Findlay for Suzuki.

⚘ THIRD TIME LUCKY FOR NORTON ⚘

Norton riders finished fifth (Artie Bell), sixth (Harold Daniell) and seventh (John Lockett) in the inaugural 500cc World Championship. In 1950, Geoff Duke's Norton was runner-up to Umberto Massetti (Gilera) despite winning three races to the Italian's two. However, in 1951, Duke gave Norton what proved to be their only 500cc crown. Nonetheless, the team had at least one rider in the 500cc World Championship top 10 every year until 1970.

❂ 350CC WORLD CHAMPIONS 1949–1982 ❂

Year	Rider (Nationality)	Bike
1949	Freddie Frith (GBR)	Velocette
1950	Bob Foster (GBR)	Velocette
1951	Geoff Duke (GBR)	Norton
1952	Geoff Duke (GBR)	Norton
1953	Fergus Anderson (GBR)	Moto Guzzi
1954	Fergus Anderson (GBR)	Moto Guzzi
1955	Bill Lomas (GBR)	Moto Guzzi
1956	Bill Lomas (GBR)	Moto Guzzi
1957	Keith Campbell (GBR)	Moto Guzzi
1958	John Surtees (GBR)	MV Agusta
1959	John Surtees (GBR)	MV Agusta
1960	John Surtees (GBR)	MV Agusta
1961	Gary Hocking (RHO)	MV Agusta
1962	Jim Redman (RHO)	Honda
1963	Jim Redman (RHO)	Honda
1964	Jim Redman (RHO)	Honda
1965	Jim Redman (RHO)	Honda
1966	Mike Hailwood (GBR)	Honda
1967	Mike Hailwood (GBR)	Honda
1968	Giacomo Agostini (ITA)	MV Agusta
1969	Giacomo Agostini (ITA)	MV Agusta
1970	Giacomo Agostini (ITA)	MV Agusta
1971	Giacomo Agostini (ITA)	MV Agusta
1972	Giacomo Agostini (ITA)	MV Agusta
1973	Giacomo Agostini (ITA)	MV Agusta
1974	Giacomo Agostini (ITA)	Yamaha
1975	Johnny Cecotto (VEN)	Yamaha
1976	Walter Villa (ITA)	Harley-Davidson
1977	Takazumi Katayama (JPN)	Yamaha
1978	Kork Ballington (RSA)	Kawasaki
1979	Kork Ballington (RSA)	Kawasaki
1980	Jon Ekerold (RSA)	Bimota-Yamaha
1981	Anton Mang (FDR)	Kawasaki
1982	Anton Mang (FDR)	Kawasaki

❂ STILL WAITING ❂

Suzuki, Yamaha and Honda may dominate the MotoGP grid, but no
Japanese rider has been 500cc/MotoGP World Champion. Japan's first
350cc World Champion was Takazumi Katayama (Yamaha) in 1977.

❀ 350CC MULTIPLE WINNERS ❀

Giacomo Agostini	7
Jim Redman	4
John Surtees	3
Geoff Duke	2
Fergus Anderson	2
Bill Lomas	2
Mike Hailwood	2
Kork Ballington	2
Anton Mang	2

❀ 350CC CONSTRUCTORS' TITLES ❀

MV Agusta	10
Honda	6
Moto Guzzi	5
Kawasaki	4
Yamaha	4
Norton	2
Velocette	2
Harley-Davidson	1

❀ DEATH AND GLORY AT THE SAME GP ❀

In 1982, the Swiss racer, Michel Frutschi, gave the small Italian bike manufacturer, Sanvenero, an unlikely victory in the 500cc French Grand Prix at Nogaro's Circuit Paul Armagnac. The following year the French GP was moved to Le Mans but it was marred by two tragedies. Japanese rider Iwao Ishikawa (Honda) died after colliding with Italy's Loris Reggiani (Suzuki) during practice and, in the 500cc race, Frutschi crashed heavily and later died in hospital.

Did You Know That?
Sanvenero was the only non-Japanese team to pick up a win or a point in the 1982 500cc World Championship.

❀ HONDA HERO ❀

Australian Tom Phillis created history for Honda when he won the 125cc Spanish Grand Prix in 1961. It was the Japanese company's first ever World Championship Grand Prix victory and Phillis went on to become that year's 125cc World Champion too.

❂ SIDECAR CHAMPIONSHIP 1949–1996 ❂

The F.I.M. Sidecar World Championship ran from 1949 to 1996.
These were the champions:

Year	Rider (Nat)	Passenger (Nat)	Maker
1949	Eric Oliver (GBR)	Denis Jenkinson (GBR)	Norton
1950	Eric Oliver (GBR)	Lorenzo Dobelli (ITA)	Norton
1951	Eric Oliver (GBR)	Lorenzo Dobelli (ITA)	Norton
1952	Cyril Smith (GBR)	Bob Clements (GBR)	
		Les Nutt (GBR)	Norton
1953	Eric Oliver (GBR)	Stanley Dibben (GBR)	Norton
1954	Wilhelm Noll (GER)	Fritz Cron (GER)	BMW
1955	Willi Faust (GER)	Karl Remmert (GER)	BMW
1956	Wilhelm Noll (GER)	Fritz Cron (GER)	BMW
1957	Fritz Hillebrand (GER)	Manfred Grunwahl (GER)	BMW
1958	Walter Schneider (GER)	Hans Strauss (GER)	BMW
1959	Walter Schneider (GER)	Hans Strauss (GER)	BMW
1960	Helmut Fath (GER)	Alfred Wohlgemuth (GER)	BMW
1961	Max Deubel (GER)	Emil Horner (GER)	BMW
1962	Max Deubel (GER)	Emil Horner (GER)	BMW
1963	Max Deubel (GER)	Emil Horner (GER)	BMW
1964	Max Deubel (GER)	Emil Horner (GER)	BMW
1965	Fritz Scheidegger (SWI)	John Robinson (GBR)	BMW
1966	Fritz Scheidegger (SWI)	John Robinson (GBR)	BMW
1967	Klaus Enders (GER)	Ralf Engelhardt (GER)	BMW
1968	Helmut Fath (GER)	Wolfgang Kalauch (GER)	URS
1969	Fritz Scheidegger (GER)	Ralf Engelhardt (GER)	BMW
1970	Fritz Scheidegger (GER)	Ralf Engelhardt (GER)	
		Wolfgang Kalauch (GER)	BMW
1971	Horst Owesle (GER)	Julius Kremer (GER)	
		Peter Rutterford (GBR)	URS
1972	Klaus Enders (GER)	Ralf Engelhardt (GER)	BMW
1973	Klaus Enders (GER)	Ralf Engelhardt (GER)	BMW
1974	Klaus Enders (GER)	Ralf Engelhardt (GER)	BMW
1975	Rolf Steinhausen (GER)	Josef Huber (GER)	Konig
1976	Rolf Steinhausen (GER)	Josef Huber (GER)	Konig
1977	George O'Dell (GBR)	Kenny Arthur (GBR)	
		Cliff Holland (GBR)	Yamaha
1978	Rolf Biland (SWI)	Kenneth Williams (GBR)	Yamaha
1979	B2A: Rolf Biland (SWI)	Kurt Waltisperg (SWI)	Yamaha
	B2B: Bruno Holzer (SWI)	Charlie Maierhans (SWI)	Yamaha
1980	Jock Taylor (GBR)	Benga Johansson (SWE)	Yamaha

1981	Rolf Biland (SWI)	Kurt Waltisperg (SWI)	Yamaha
1982	Werner Schwärtzel (GER)	Andreas Huber (GER)	Yamaha
1983	Rolf Biland (SWI)	Kurt Waltisperg (SWI)	Yamaha
1984	Egbert Streuer (NED)	Bernie Schnieders (NED)	Yamaha
1985	Egbert Streuer (NED)	Bernie Schnieders (NED)	Yamaha
1986	Egbert Streuer (NED)	Bernie Schnieders (NED)	Yamaha
1987	Steve Webster (GBR)	Tony Hewitt (GBR)	Krauser
1988	Steve Webster (GBR)	Tony Hewitt (GBR) Gavin Simmons (GBR)	Krauser
1989	Steve Webster (GBR)	Tony Hewitt (GBR)	Krauser
1990	Alain Michel (FRA)	Simon Birchall (GBR)	Krauser
1991	Steve Webster (GBR)	Gavin Simmons (GBR)	Krauser
1992	Rolf Biland (SWI)	Kurt Waltisperg (SWI)	Krauser
1993	Rolf Biland (SWI)	Kurt Waltisperg (SWI)	Krauser
1994	Rolf Biland (SWI)	Kurt Waltisperg (SWI)	Swissauto
1995	Darren Dixon (GBR)	Andy Hetherington (GBR)	ADM
1996	Darren Dixon (GBR)	Andy Hetherington (GBR)	ADM

Did You Know That?
The 1979 Sidecar World Championship was split into two classes.

◉ 1975 500CC FINAL STANDINGS (TOP 10) ◉

Pos	Rider	Nationality	Bike	Pts
1.	Giacomo Agostini	(ITA)	Yamaha	84
2.	Phil Read	(GBR)	MV Agusta	76
3.	Hideo Kanaya	(JPN)	Yamaha	45
4.	Teuvo Lansivuori	(FIN)	Suzuki	40
5.	John Williams	(GBR)	Yamaha	32
6.	Barry Sheene	(GBR)	Yamaha	30
=	Alex George	(GBR)	Yamaha	30
8.	John Newbold	(GBR)	Suzuki	24
=	Armando Toracca	(ITA)	MV Agusta	24
10.	Jack Findlay	(AUS)	Suzuki	23

◉ CONSTRUCTORS' FINAL STANDINGS (TOP 5) ◉

Pos	Team	Nationality	Pts
1.	Yamaha	(JPN)	131
2.	MV Agusta	(ITA)	96
3.	Suzuki	(JPN)	86
4.	Kawasaki	(JPN)	15
=	Konig	(GER)	15

● 1976 500CC FINAL STANDINGS (TOP 10) ●

Pos	Rider	Nationality	Bike	Pts
1.	Barry Sheene	(GBR)	Suzuki	72
2.	Teuvo Lansivuori	(FIN)	Suzuki	48
3.	Pat Hennen	(USA)	Suzuki	46
4.	Marco Lucchinelli	(ITA)	Suzuki	40
5.	John Newbold	(GBR)	Suzuki	31
6.	Philippe Coulon	(SUI)	Suzuki	28
7.	Giacomo Agostini	(ITA)	Suzuki/MV Agusta	26
8.	Jack Findlay	(AUS)	Suzuki	25
9.	John Williams	(GBR)	Suzuki	24
10.	Phil Read	(GBR)	Suzuki	22

● CONSTRUCTORS' FINAL STANDINGS (TOP 3) ●

Pos	Team	Nationality	Pts
1.	Suzuki	(JPN)	136
2.	Yamaha	(JPN)	53
3.	MV Agusta	(ITA)	26

● LADIES OF THE TRACK ●

Only nine women have ridden in the F.I.M. World Championship. Inga Stoll was a sidecar passenger in the 1950s, until she died in a crash. Beryl Swain rode in the Isle of Man TT 50cc race in 1962, but was forced to retire after a minimum weight requirement was introduced. The only woman to ride in the 500cc class, Gina Bovaird, from Boston, USA, qualified for the 1982 French Grand Prix but neither finished nor qualified for another 500cc World Championship race. German rider Katya Poensgen is the only woman to score points in the 250ccc World Championship, collecting two in the 2001 Italian Grand Prix. Tomoko Igata of Japan (30 points) and Finland's Taru Rinne (25) enjoyed some success in the 125cc class, while in Moto2, Elena Rossell of Spain rode in 2011 and 2012 without success. Two Spaniards were in MotoGP in 2015. Maria Herrera finished 29th overall with nine points, while Ana Carrasco earned nine points in her rookie season, 2013.

● FAST TALK (7) ●

"You live more for five minutes going fast on a bike
than other people do in all of their life."
Marco Simoncelli

🏍 GREATEST RACES (5) – 1992 BRITISH GP 🏍

Wayne Gardner was involved in many battles in his 10-year track career. The popular Australian, 500cc World Champion in 1987 and runner-up in 1988, had decided 1992 would be his last season. Although fourth on the grid – behind Eddie Lawson (Cagiva), John Kocinski (Yamaha) and Wayne Rainey (Yamaha) – his British GP victory hopes were considered slim.

In very wet conditions, Kocinski made a superb start, but was behind Rainey, Lawson and Kevin Schwantz (Suzuki) by the end of the opening lap. Gardner, however, had slid off into the mud at the Esses. He got back on his bike and, forever the racer, set off after the field.

Within two laps, he had charged past four rivals and, not long after that, Gardner was leading the race. Schwantz, however, regained first place after passing him at the Old Hairpin and led for several laps before Gardner passed him again at the Chicane. Schwantz was then overtaken by Rainey at Redgate but, with five laps remaining, crashed at Redgate. Gardner took the chequered flag, almost a second clear of Rainey for his 18th and final victory.

1992 British Grand Prix – Silverstone – Sunday 2 August

Pos	Pts	Rider (Nationality)	Bike	Time/Gap
1.	20	Wayne Gardner (AUS)	Honda	47m 38.373s
2.	15	Wayne Rainey (USA)	Yamaha	+0.855s
3.	12	Juan Garriga (SPA)	Yamaha	+5.915s
4.	10	Eddie Lawson (USA)	Cagiva	+26.079s
5.	8	Peter Goddard (AUS)	Yamaha	+1m 01.091ss

Did You Know That?
One commentator likened Gardner's performance (he was nicknamed "The Wild One") in the 1992 500cc British GP to that of John Wayne's lead character in the movie *Rooster Cogburn*.

🏍 IT WAS A LONG TIME AGO 🏍

The 2015 Moto3 World Champion was Danny Kent, born in Chippenham, Wiltshire, on 25 November 1993. He was the first British winner of an F.I.M. World Championship since Barry Sheene was 500cc World Champion in 1977. To put this gap into perspective, the last 500cc World Champion to have been alive when Barry clinched that title was the then four-year-old son of one of Sheene's biggest rivals Kenny Roberts Jr (son of King Kenny), who won in 2000.

❃ BARRY SHEENE MBE – THE BIONIC MAN ❃

Barry Sheene was a brilliant, if maverick, motorcycle racing superstar, the first to be globally recognized. He was the quintessential racer: a charismatic, exuberant playboy, with good looks and a cheeky grin; he drove a Rolls-Royce and owned a helicopter. But, most of all, he was dedicated to his sport and had the speed on the track to win two successive 500cc World Championships for Suzuki in 1977 and 1978. Barry was born on 11 September 1950 in central London. His father Frank was a resident surgeon and a former motorcycle racer, so motorcycle racing was in his blood. He followed in his father's footsteps – he actually started riding bikes aged five – and, after leaving school, was a messenger and delivery rider.

His prodigious talent was evident when, as a 17-year-old in 1968, Barry won on his dad's 125cc and 250cc Bultacos at Brands Hatch. Three years later, he finished runner-up, by eight points, behind Angel Nieto in the 125cc World Championship, his first win coming in the Belgian GP at the famous Spa circuit, but also finished seventh overall in the 500cc World Championship and won the Czechoslovakian GP at Brno – he was more than two and a half minutes ahead of the second-placed rider. His success persuaded the Yamaha works team to sign him to race for them in the 1972 250cc World Championship. However, a tirade about the bike's performance after Round 3, the Austrian GP, saw him dropped from the team – and his replacement Jarno Saarinen won the 125cc World Championship.

Suzuki signed Barry for the 1973 season and he won the new Formula 750 European Championship. A year later, on the new RG500, he finished sixth in the 500cc World Championship. His first major mishap came in March 1975, in practice for the Daytona 200 in America, crashing at 170mph and breaking his collarbone, arm, thigh and six ribs – career-threatening injuries. Barry was riding again seven weeks later and, on 28 June, he won his first 500cc, the Dutch GP, at Assen. He dominated the 1976 season, winning the opening GP at Le Mans, France, and four others to become the 500cc World Champion.

Barry went one better in 1977, winning six Grands Prix on his way to retaining the 500cc World Championship. It would be his last World Championship, finishing runner-up behind Kenny Roberts (Yamaha) in both 1978 and 1979. Feeling the Suzuki was not fast enough, Barry left the company and rode a privately-entered Yamaha. He finished 15th in the championship, but bounced back on a more competitive Yamaha in 1981, finishing fourth overall. Another fearsome crash in practice, for the 1982 British GP at Silverstone, left him with a multiply-fractured leg and fears he might never walk again. Once more, he bounced back, but was not competitive and retired after the 1984 season. He moved to Australia in 1987 (the climate being better for his arthritis) but, sadly, he did not enjoy a long retirement, dying from cancer – a legacy of his smoking habit – aged 52, on 10 March 2003. He left a widow, former *Penthouse* magazine model Stephanie McLean, a son and a daughter.

Did You Know That?
Barry had a hole drilled through the chin-bar on his full-face helmet allowing him to smoke right up to the start of a race.

● 1977 500CC FINAL STANDINGS (TOP 10) ●

Pos	Rider	Nationality	Bike	Pts
1.	Barry Sheene	(GBR)	Suzuki	107
2.	Steve Baker	(USA)	Yamaha	80
3.	Pat Hennen	(USA)	Suzuki	67
4.	Johnny Cecotto	(VEN)	Yamaha	50
5.	Steve Parrish	(GBR)	Suzuki	39
6.	Giacomo Agostini	(ITA)	Yamaha	37
=	Franco Bonera	(ITA)	Suzuki	37
8.	Philippe Coulon	(SUI)	Suzuki	36
9.	Teuvo Lansivuori	(FIN)	Suzuki	35
10.	Wil Hartog	(NED)	Suzuki	30

● CONSTRUCTORS' FINAL STANDINGS (TOP 2) ●

Pos	Team	Nationality	Pts
1.	Suzuki	(JPN)	157
2.	Yamaha	(JPN)	114

● NICE WORK – IF YOU CAN GET IT ●

Valentino Rossi was the world's highest-earning motorcycle racer in 2015, raking in $15 to $20 million per year in salary and endorsement deals. Rossi is the only MotoGP star who regularly features in *Forbes Top 100* highest-paid athletes in the world. It is estimated that in 2007, after he had won his fifth MotoGP World Championship, Rossi was earning approximately $35 million a year in salary and endorsements combined.

Did You Know That?
By comparison, four F1 drivers made the *Forbes* top 50 list in 2015, Lewis Hamilton, Sebastian Vettel, Kimi Raikkonen and Fernando Alonso.

⚙ 1978 500CC FINAL STANDINGS (TOP 10) ⚙

Pos	Rider	Nationality	Bike	Pts
1.	Kenny Roberts	(USA)	Yamaha	110
2.	Barry Sheene	(GBR)	Suzuki	100
3.	Johnny Cecotto	(VEN)	Yamaha	66
4.	Wil Hartog	(NED)	Suzuki	65
5.	Takazumi Katayama	(JPN)	Yamaha	53
6.	Pat Hennen	(USA)	Suzuki	51
7.	Steve Baker	(USA)	Suzuki	42
8.	Teuvo Lansivuori	(FIN)	Suzuki	39
9.	Marco Lucchinelli	(ITA)	Suzuki	30
10.	Michel Rougerie	(FRA)	Suzuki	23

⚙ CONSTRUCTORS' FINAL STANDINGS (TOP 2) ⚙

Pos	Team	Nationality	Pts
1.	Suzuki	(JPN)	146
2.	Yamaha	(JPN)	139

⚙ FAST TALK (8) ⚙

"Your ambition outweighs your talent."
*Casey Stoner speaking about Valentino Rossi after being
taken out of the 2011 Spanish Grand Prix by Rossi
who was "chancing" a risky passing manoeuvre*

⚙ 1966 – A GOOD YEAR FOR HONDA ⚙

Honda completed a unique clean sweep of all five Motorcycling Grand Prix World Championship Manufacturers' titles in 1966, 50cc, 125cc, 250cc, 350cc and 500cc. In addition, two Honda riders won three of the World Championships: Mike Hailwood took the 250cc and 350cc titles – he also finished second behind MV Agusta's Giacomo Agostini in the 500cc class – and Luigi Taveri claimed the 125cc crown. In the 50cc World Championship, Honda's George Bryans finished two points behind Hans-Georg Anscheidt of Suzuki.

⚙ AN EXPENSIVE RIDE ⚙

Marc Marquez's bike, on which he was 2013 and 2014 MotoGP World Champion, a Honda RC213V, is estimated to have cost $2 million to manufacture. A street version of the bike costs a mere $184,000!

❀ THE ISLE OF MAN TT ❀

Between 1949 and 1976, the Isle of Man Senior TT (Tourist Trophy) race formed part of the 500cc Motorcycle Racing World Championship, but its history goes back more than a century, to 1907. More than 300 riders have taken the chequered flag at an Isle of Man TT race in the various classes (there were eight in 2015) including a number of 500cc Motorcycle Racing World Champions. Giacomo Agostini made his TT debut in 1965 and secured a podium finish, third place in the Junior TT on a MV Agusta. The following year he claimed the first of his 10 TT wins, all of which were for the Italian team, in the Junior TT. He also set a new lap record in the Senior TT on his way to finishing second behind Honda's Mike Hailwood. Over the following six years, Agostini firmly established himself as an Isle of Man TT great, winning four more 350cc races and five – consecutively – in the Senior 500cc class. That last victory, in 1972, was also his last appearance at the Isle of Man following the death of his good friend and compatriot Gilberto Parlotti in the 125cc race. Agostini may well have overtaken Hailwood (14 wins), the fourth most successful rider in Isle of Man TT Racing history, if he had returned to the island in the final five seasons of his career. The three men ahead of Hailwood are Dave Molyneaux, 17 wins, John McGuinness, 21, and the legendary Joey Dunlop, 26. Joey, from Ballymoney, Northern Ireland, won a staggering seven Formula One TT, five Ultra-Lightweight, four each in the Lightweight and Senior TT, three Junior TT, one each in the Classic and Jubilee Lightweight 250 TT.

Did You Know That?

The Snaefell Mountain Course is one of the most complicated and difficult circuits in all motorsport. Raced on the roads of the Isle of Man, a lap covers more than 37 miles (60km), goes from sea level to 1,300 feet (396m) and there are around 200 corners, bends or kinks to navigate around. Tragically, there have been 141 competitor fatalities in the 96 editions of the Isle of Man TT – and 250 in all events (including two on the parade lap). In addition 12 spectators or officials have also perished.

❀ FERRARI IS FIRST PRIZE ❀

The small Italian team Cagiva Corse created a stir when they signed four-times 500cc World Champion Eddie Lawson to ride for them in the 1991 season. When "Steady Eddie" won the 1992 Hungarian Grand Prix, Cagiva Corse's first top-class victory, it is rumoured his reward from the team for that race victory was a brand-new Ferrari.

◉ 1979 500CC FINAL STANDINGS (TOP 10) ◉

Pos	Rider	Nationality	Bike	Pts
1.	Kenny Roberts	(USA)	Yamaha	113
2.	Virginio Ferrari	(ITA)	Suzuki	89
3.	Barry Sheene	(GBR)	Suzuki	87
4.	Wil Hartog	(NED)	Suzuki	66
5.	Franco Uncini	(ITA)	Suzuki	51
6.	Boet van Dulmen	(NED)	Suzuki	50
7.	Jack Middelburg	(NED)	Suzuki	42
8.	Randy Mamola	(USA)	Suzuki	29
=	Philippe Coulon	(SUI)	Suzuki	29
10.	Tom Herron	(NIR)	Suzuki	28

◉ CONSTRUCTORS' FINAL STANDINGS (TOP 3) ◉

Pos	Team	Nationality	Pts
1.	Suzuki	(JPN)	165
2.	Yamaha	(JPN)	130
3.	Morbidelli	(ITA)	2

◉ THE FOX ◉

Nine-times World Champion Carlo Ubbiali (three wins in the 250cc class, six in 125cc), who raced in the early years of the F.I.M. World Championship (1950–60), was one of the most tactically astute racers in the sport's history, earning the nickname, "The Fox". He would regularly engage in race-long duels with a rival, only to pull away to win on the final lap. "Track safety" was pretty much an oxymoron in those days, but Ubbiali was so clever that he never had a major crash in a World Championship Grand Prix. He proved riders never lose that instinct at the Assen Centennial Classic in 1998, a nostalgic celebration of the first four decades of Grand Prix racing, when, aged 68, he easily won his class.

◉ IN BARRY SHEENE'S SLIPSTREAM ◉

During the 2012 Spanish Grand Prix at the Circuito de Jerez, Cal Crutchlow set the fastest lap of the race, covering the 2.748 miles (4.423 km) in 1min 40.019secs. This was the first time in 28 years that a British rider had set the fastest lap in a 500cc/MotoGP World Championship race. The previous fastest lap had been Barry Sheene, riding a Suzuki at the 1984 South African Grand Prix at Kyalami.

❂ FANTASY 500CC/MOTOGP
EUROPEAN STARTING GRID ❂

(to the end of the 2015 season)

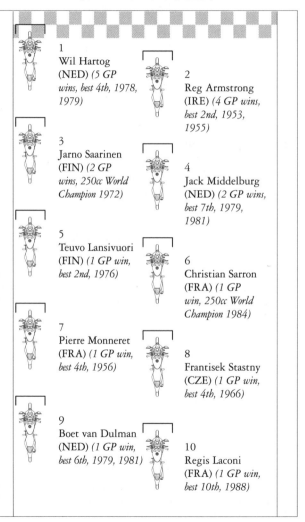

1
Wil Hartog
(NED) *(5 GP wins, best 4th, 1978, 1979)*

2
Reg Armstrong
(IRE) *(4 GP wins, best 2nd, 1953, 1955)*

3
Jarno Saarinen
(FIN) *(2 GP wins, 250cc World Champion 1972)*

4
Jack Middelburg
(NED) *(2 GP wins, best 7th, 1979, 1981)*

5
Teuvo Lansivuori
(FIN) *(1 GP win, best 2nd, 1976)*

6
Christian Sarron
(FRA) *(1 GP win, 250cc World Champion 1984)*

7
Pierre Monneret
(FRA) *(1 GP win, best 4th, 1956)*

8
Frantisek Stastny
(CZE) *(1 GP win, best 4th, 1966)*

9
Boet van Dulman
(NED) *(1 GP win, best 6th, 1979, 1981)*

10
Regis Laconi
(FRA) *(1 GP win, best 10th, 1988)*

⚜ 1980 500CC FINAL STANDINGS (TOP 10) ⚜

Pos	Rider	Nationality	Bike	Pts
1.	Kenny Roberts	(USA)	Yamaha	87
2.	Randy Mamola	(USA)	Suzuki	72
3.	Marco Lucchinelli	(ITA)	Suzuki	59
4.	Franco Uncini	(ITA)	Suzuki	50
5.	Graziano Rossi	(ITA)	Suzuki	38
6.	Wil Hartog	(NED)	Suzuki	31
=	Johnny Cecotto	(VEN)	Yamaha	31
8.	Graeme Crosby	(NZL)	Suzuki	29
9.	Jack Middelburg	(NED)	Suzuki	20
10.	Takazumi Katayama	(JPN)	Suzuki	18

⚜ CONSTRUCTORS' FINAL STANDINGS (TOP 3) ⚜

Pos	Team	Nationality	Pts
1.	Suzuki	(JPN)	108
2.	Yamaha	(JPN)	102
3.	Kawasaki	(JPN)	13

⚜ WHEN HOME IS NOT HOME ⚜

On 13 September 1987, the inaugural 500cc Portuguese Grand Prix was staged, even though it was not in Portugal, but at the Circuito del Jarama in Jerez, Spain. The reason the race – won by Eddie Lawson riding a Yamaha – was held in Spain was that the race organizers had transferred their rights to the Jarama organizers. It would be 13 years before the Portuguese GP returned but, in 2000, the race was held on home soil at the Autodromo do Estoril. Once more, a Yamaha rider would take the 500cc chequered flag, this time Australian racer Garry McCoy.

Did You Know That?
Garry McCoy won only five World Championship Grands Prix in his 15-year career. He won one 125cc race in both 1995 and 1996 and three 500cc races in 2000.

⚜ A BRITISH DOMAIN ⚜

Until Max Biaggi in 2010, only one non-British European racer had been Superbikes World Champion, Raymond Roche of France in 1990. No Briton had been F.I.M. World Champion – in any class – since 1977.

❀ 250CC WORLD CHAMPIONS 1949–2009 ❀

The 250cc World Championship was contested from 1949 to 2009, after which it was renamed Moto2. Thesse were the winners of the 250cc World Championship in those 61 seasons:

Year	Rider (Nationality)	Year	Rider (Nationality)
1949	Bruno Ruffo (ITA)	1980	Anton Mang (GER)
1950	Dario Ambrosini (ITA)	1981	Anton Mang (GER)
1951	Bruno Ruffo (ITA)	1982	Jean-Louis Tournadre (FRA)
1952	Enrico Lorenzetti (ITA)	1983	Carlos Lavado (VEN)
1953	Werner Haas (GER)	1984	Christian Sarron (FRA)
1954	Werner Haas (GER)	1985	Freddie Spencer (USA)
1955	Herman Paul Muller (GER)	1986	Carlos Lavado (VEN)
1956	Carlio Ubbiali (ITA)	1987	Anton Mang (GER)
1957	Cecil Sandford (GBR)	1988	Sito Pons (ESP)
1958	Tarquino Provini (ITA)	1989	Sito Pons (ESP)
1959	Carlio Ubbiali (ITA)	1990	John Kocinski (USA)
1960	Carlo Ubbiali (ITA)	1991	Luca Cadalora (ITA)
1961	Mike Hailwood (GBR)	1992	Luca Cadalora (ITA)
1962	Jim Redman (RHO)	1993	Tetsuya Harada (JAP)
1963	Jim Redman (RHO)	1994	Max Biaggi (ITA)
1964	Phil Read (GBR)	1995	Max Biaggi (ITA)
1965	Phil Read (GBR)	1996	Max Biaggi (ITA)
1966	Mike Hailwood (GBR)	1997	Max Biaggi (ITA)
1967	Mike Hailwood (GBR)	1998	Loris Capirossi (ITA)
1968	Phil Read (GBR)	1999	Valentino Rossi (ITA)
1969	Kel Carruthers (AUS)	2000	Olivier Jacque (FRA)
1970	Rodney Gould (GBR)	2001	Daijiro Kato (JAP)
1971	Phil Read (GBR)	2002	Marco Melandri (ITA)
1972	Jarno Saarinen (FIN)	2003	Manuel Poggiali (SMO)
1973	Dieter Braun (GER)	2004	Dani Pedrosa (ESP)
1974	Walter Villa (ITA)	2005	Dani Pedrosa (ESP)
1975	Walter Villa (ITA)	2006	Jorge Lorenzo (ESP)
1976	Walter Villa (ITA)	2007	Jorge Lorenzo (ESP)
1977	Mario Lega (ITA)	2008	Marco Simoncelli (ITA)
1978	Kork Ballington (RSA)	2009	Hiroshi Aoyama (JAP)
1979	Kork Ballington (RSA)		

Did You Know That?

A number of racers won World Championships in different classes in the same season, but Freddie Spencer, in 1985, is the only man to win the 500cc and 250cc World Championship in the same year.

⚙ 1981 500CC FINAL STANDINGS (TOP 10) ⚙

Pos	Rider	Nationality	Bike	Pts
1.	Marco Lucchinelli	(ITA)	Suzuki	105
2.	Randy Mamola	(USA)	Suzuki	94
3.	Kenny Roberts	(USA)	Yamaha	74
4.	Barry Sheene	(GBR)	Yamaha	72
5.	Graeme Crosby	(NZL)	Suzuki	68
6.	Boet van Dulmen	(NED)	Yamaha	64
7.	Jack Middelburg	(NED)	Suzuki	60
8.	Kork Ballington	(RSA)	Kawasaki	43
9.	Marc Fontan	(FRA)	Yamaha	25
10.	Hiroyuki Kawasaki	(JPN)	Suzuki	19

⚙ CONSTRUCTORS' FINAL STANDINGS (TOP 3) ⚙

Pos	Team	Nationality	Pts
1.	Suzuki	(JPN)	152
2.	Yamaha	(JPN)	123
3.	Kawasaki	(JPN)	43

⚙ IANNONE HEADBUTTS SEAGULL ⚙

On 18 October 2015, on the second lap of the 2015 Australian Grand Prix, a seagull landed on the Philip Island track. Ducati rider Andrea Iannone was leading the race and as he turned the corner the bird flew up into the air and ended up flying into the Italian racer's helmet. Iannone, who has yet to win a race in MotoGP, was able to continue and eventually finished third, behind the Spanish duo of Marc Marquez and Jorge Lorenzo, but ahead of compatriot Valentino Rossi.

Did You Know That?
Lorenzo (first), Rossi (second) and Marquez (third), along with fourth-placed Spaniard Dani Pedrosa were the only ones to finish ahead of Iannone in the final 2015 MotoGP World Championship standings.

⚙ GO COMPARE ⚙

Mark Marquez, is frequently compared with the winner of 15 World Championships, in all classes, Valentino Rossi. Both racers ride to the limit and both have won World Championships in three different classes: Rossi 125cc, 250cc and 500cc/MotoGP, Marquez 125cc (in 2010), Moto2 (2012) & MotoGP (2013 and 2014).

❂ NOT SO CLOSE ❂

In 1969, a Swiss racer of Hungarian descent, Gyula Marsovszky, finished second – albeit a long way behind, 47 points to 105 – to Giacomo Agostini in the 500cc World Championship. It was an improvement, because in 1968, he had finished third in the table, behind the Italian and Australia's Jack Findlay, having mustered only 10 points. In both seasons, Agostini won every race he entered, all 10 in 1968 and the first 10 in 1969 – he didn't race in the Ulster Grand Prix and did not start the season-ending Yugoslavia GP. Marsovszky rode a Linto bike in 1969, having been on a Seeley-Matchless machine the year before. In his career, Marsovszky won only one Grand Prix; it was the 1971 250cc Nations GP at Monza and he was riding a Yamaha.

❂ JOINED TOGETHER ❂

The Linto 500 bike was created by Lino Tonti (Lin-To), an engineer from Romagna, Italy, in the late 1960s. The 500cc bike was designed between 1967 and 1968 and it was powered by two joined-together 250 single-cylinder Aermacchi horizontal engines.

❂ ALLEZ FRANCE ❂

The first 500cc World Championship French Grand Prix was at Albi on 14 July 1951 and it was won by an Italian, Alfredo Milani. There was no World Championship race in 1952, but in 1953, at Rouen-Les-Essarts, Britain's Geoff Duke took the 500cc French GP. A year later the home fans, this time at Reims, were cheering one of their own, as Pierre Monneret led everyone home. The only other time, since then, that a French rider has won the 500cc French GP was at Pau in 1958 when Jacques Collot took the chequered flag. Unfortunately, it was a year when the race was not part of the World Championship. Apart from 1993, the French 500cc/MotoGP race has been part of the World Championship calendar every year since 1972.

❂ F.I.M. ❂

The Federation Internationale de Motocyclisme (F.I.M.) began life in 1949 when the Federation Internationale des Clubs Motocyclistes (F.I.C.M.) was rebranded. The F.I.C.M., the first international motorbike federation, had been founded in 1904, in Paris, but it was dissolved in 1906, only to re-form in 1912, based in England.

● 1982 500CC FINAL STANDINGS (TOP 10) ●

Pos	Rider	Nationality	Bike	Pts
1.	Franco Uncini	(ITA)	Suzuki	103
2.	Graeme Crosby	(NZL)	Yamaha	76
3.	Freddie Spencer	(USA)	Honda	72
4.	Kenny Roberts	(USA)	Yamaha	68
=	Barry Sheene	(GBR)	Yamaha	68
6.	Randy Mamola	(USA)	Suzuki	65
7.	Takazumi Katayama	(JPN)	Honda	48
8.	Marco Lucchinelli	(ITA)	Honda	48
9.	Kork Ballington	(RSA)	Kawasaki	31
10.	Marc Fontan	(FRA)	Yamaha	29

● CONSTRUCTORS' FINAL STANDINGS (TOP 5) ●

Pos	Team	Nationality	Pts
1.	Suzuki	(JPN)	154
2.	Yamaha	(JPN)	128
3.	Honda	(JPN)	104
4.	Kawasaki	(JPN)	36
5.	Sanvenero	(ITA)	17

● FAST TALK (9) ●

"Don't wait for your ship to come in, swim out and
meet the bloody thing."
Barry Sheene

● WISH YOU WERE HERE ●

Valentino Rossi paid an emotional and heartfelt tribute to his late
friend Marco Simoncelli at the 2013 San Marino Grand Prix held at
the renamed Misano World Circuit Marco Simoncelli, close to the
pair's birthplaces. Rossi commissioned a special racing helmet that
featured the artwork and lyrics from Pink Floyd's song "Wish You
Were Here".

Did You Know That?
Wish You Were Here was the name of Pink Floyd's ninth studio album
released in 1975. Track No.25 on their 2001 album *Echoes: The Best
of Pink Floyd* is the single "Wish You Were Here", and it seems most
fitting as Marco died just a few months short of his 25th birthday.

❧ LEAVING THE SILK ROAD ❧

In October 1909, Michio Suzuki founded the Suzuki Loom Works in Hamamatsu, Japan. The company made weaving looms for Japan's burgeoning silk industry and it wasn't until 1952 that Suzuki entered the motor-vehicle arena, when they launched its Power Free 36cc motorized bicycle. Less than a year later, Suzuki debuted its Diamond Free 60cc 2-cycle motorized bicycle, producing 6,000 bikes a month. Today, Suzuki also builds cars, marine engines, trucks and wheelchairs.

❧ INCIDENT-PACKED SEASON-OPENER ❧

The opening race on the 1990 500cc World Championship calendar was the Japanese Grand Prix at Suzuka. Wayne Rainey set the fastest ever lap at Suzuka in qualifying, his 2 minutes, 09.589 seconds being the first sub-2 minutes, 10 seconds. However, the race was packed full of incident. On Lap 4, Michael Doohan lost control of his Honda braking going into 130R; it caused his back wheel to rise, he lost the front end, and his back wheel then caught Eddie Lawson's Yamaha, causing both to crash out of the race. Going into the final lap Rainey had the race won, leaving Wayne Gardner (Honda) and Kevin Schwantz (Suzuki) to battle it out for second place. As they went into the final chicane, Gardner drifted slightly wide resulting in Schwantz touching the back wheel of the Honda and ending up dropping his bike on the track. The pair had taken the corner at a slow speed which meant Schwantz was relatively unscathed as he was able to get back on his bike and still finish third.

❧ A LOT MORE SPACE ❧

In 1990, the F.I.M. changed the regulations for the starting grid in the various classes of the Motorcycle World Championship. With the speed of the bikes continuing to grow, they decided that instead of five riders abreast racing towards the first corner, there would now be only four with the aim of reducing the chances of crashes. Fourteen years later, MotoGP regulations reduced the number of the starting grid to three, though four remained for the two lesser classes, 250cc and 125cc. By a strange coincidence, the pole-setters in both 1990 and 2004 went on to win the season-opener, Wayne Rainey at the Japanese Grand Prix and Valentino Rossi at the South African GP, respectively. It was a different story for the two men who were second on the grid, because they were beaten into third place on the podium by the men who started third, Wayne Gardner getting the better of Kevin Schwantz in 1990 and Max Biaggi beating Sete Gibernau in 2004.

◉ KENNY ROBERTS – KING KENNY ◉

Kenneth (Kenny) Leroy Roberts Sr was born on 31 December 1951 in Modesto, California. He was more interested in riding horses than bikes until, aged 12, a friend dared him to ride a minibike. Instantly hooked and loving the thrill, Kenny actually built the first motorbike he ever owned, taking the engine out of his father's lawnmower and attaching it to his bicycle. A natural racer, the 16-year-old won many local dirt track races and attracted the attention of Bud Aksland, owner of a Suzuki dealership. Kenny turned professional on his 18th birthday and the next day finished fourth in a race at San Francisco's Cow Palace.

Aksland knew Kenny was a champion in the making and asked a former amateur racer Jim Doyle to become his manager. After Triumph had turned down the chance to sign Kenny for the 1971 season, he signed for Yamaha as a US-based factory-sponsored rider, alongside 1969 250cc World Champion, Kel Carruthers. Kenny, the 1971 American Motorcyclist Association Rookie of the Year, won his first race as a professional in the following year. Although a natural on dirt tracks, Kenny was less sure on the roads, particularly when cornering, but after watching Jarno Saarinen, the 1972 250cc World Champion, win the 1973 Daytona 200, he learned to shift his body weight towards the inside of a turn on the roads. Twelve months later, Kenny finished second behind seven-time 500cc World Champion Giacomo Agostini in the Daytona 200. His first 250cc World Championship race was also in 1974, a fourth-place finish in the Dutch TT at Assen.

Kenny's first season in the 500cc World Championship was in 1978 and he made a spectacular debut, outduelling Barry Sheene to win the title, the first rookie to do so. Italy's Virginio Ferrari made it a three-way battle for the 1979 World Championship, but Kenny (five wins) prevailed, ahead of Ferrari (one win) and Sheene (three wins). In 1980, "King Kenny" won the first three races on his way to completing a hat-trick of 500cc World Championships. He slipped to third in 1981 and fourth a year later, behind Italian champions Marco Luccinelli and Franco Uncini.

Kenny's final year in the saddle, 1983, saw him battle for the title with Freddie Spencer in one of the most dramatic 500cc World Championships. It came down to the final race, the San Marino GP at Imola, but Spencer, who claimed pole, had a five-point lead and needed only a top-three finish for the title. Kenny won his 22nd and final 500cc race, but Spencer was right behind him in second place, so took the title by two points (144–142).

In retirement, Kenny became a team owner and his Marlboro Yamaha-Roberts team won the 1990 250cc World Championship with John Kocinski. In 2000, Kenny Roberts Jr won the 500cc World

Championship – two years after he had left his father's team to ride for Suzuki – but the Robertses remain the only father–son combination to both win the 500cc World Championship.

Did You Know That?
Kenny always considered himself to be first and foremost a dirt-track racer. Every 500cc World Champion between 1983 and 1999 had a dirt-track background.

❀ 1983 500CC FINAL STANDINGS (TOP 10) ❀

Pos	Rider	Nationality	Bike	Pts
1.	Freddie Spencer	(USA)	Honda	144
2.	Kenny Roberts	(USA)	Yamaha	142
3.	Randy Mamola	(USA)	Suzuki	89
4.	Eddie Lawson	(USA)	Yamaha	78
5.	Takazumi Katayama	(JPN)	Honda	77
6.	Marc Fontan	(FRA)	Yamaha	64
7.	Marco Lucchinelli	(ITA)	Honda	48
8.	Ron Haslam	(GBR)	Honda	31
=	Franco Uncini	(ITA)	Suzuki	21
10.	Raymond Roche	(FRA)	Honda	22

❀ CONSTRUCTORS' FINAL STANDINGS (TOP 3) ❀

Pos	Team	Nationality	Pts
1.	Honda	(JPN)	158
2.	Yamaha	(JPN)	154
3.	Suzuki	(JPN)	100

❀ TOURIST TROPHY TROUBLES ❀

Gary Hocking was the 1961 350cc and 500cc World Champion. That year he contested 15 Grands Prix, in 250cc, 350cc and 500cc classes, and he won every race he entered, apart from the three in the Isle of Man TT series. He failed to score in the 250cc and 500cc events and Phil Read beat him into second place in the 350cc race.

Did You Know That?
Hocking collected maximum points in both World Championship classes because the 350cc counted only the best four results and the 500cc the bext six.

● GREATEST RACES (6) - 2006 PORTUGUESE GP ●

A dictionary describes "epic" as a work portraying heroic deeds or adventures. In MotoGP terms, the 2006 Portuguese Grand Prix at Estoril was an epic. It was the penultimate race of a 17-round season which had produced one of the closest, exciting, thrilling and fiercest battles ever. Five-time World Champion Valentino Rossi (Yamaha) was sitting on pole, looking for a fifth Portuguese GP and sixth win of the season. He raced away, followed by team-mate Colin Edwards, though the latter quickly fell behind Dani Pedrosa and Nicky Hayden (both Honda). On lap two, Casey Stoner (Honda) crashed and forced out Sete Gibernau (Ducati) and, three laps later, Pedrosa went off and brought down Hayden.

Profiting from these accidents was Tony Elias (Honda) who, after snatching second from Edwards, set off after Rossi. Kenny Roberts Jr also overtook Edwards to set up a thrilling three-way battle. At the final chicane, turns 9 and 10, Rossi passed Roberts Jr and Elias, but Elias came out of Rossi's slipstream at the Parabolica, the final corner, and beat the Italian by 0.002 seconds for his maiden MotoGP victory.

2006 Portuguese Grand Prix – Estoril – Sunday 15 October

Pos	Pts	Rider (Nationality)	Bike	Time/Gap
1.	25	Toni Elias (SPA)	Honda	44m 30.727s
2.	20	Valentino Rossi (ITA)	Yamaha	+0.002s
3.	16	Kenny Roberts Jr (USA)	KR211V	+0.176s
4.	13	Colin Edwards (USA)	Yamaha	+0.864s
5.	11	Makoto Tamada (JPN)	Honda	+18.419s

Did You Know That?
The five points between winner and runner-up denied Valentino Rossi a sixth consecutive world title. A 13th-place finish in the season-ending race in Valencia, coupled with Nicky Hayden's third place, gave the American the World Championship by five points. If he had won in Estoril, Rossi would have been World Champion on the tie-break (five race wins to two).

● AGO IS PIPPED ●

Giacomo Agostini was denied a debut 350cc World Championship in 1965 when Jim Redman pipped him by five points. If Ago had finished ahead of Redman in the season finale at Suzuka, Japan, he would have won the title, but his Honda had mechanical problems and he finished fifth, three places behind Redman.

☻ FAST TALK (10) ☻

*"I respect him a lot, I'll always say it. I'd like to be like him
in the future, but it will be really difficult."*
*Marc Marquez pays tribute to his great rival
Valentino Rossi in 2014*

☻ RIGHT IN ROSSI'S WHEELHOUSE ☻

The South African Grand Prix at Phasika Freeway in Welkom, South
Africa, was part of the World Motorcycle Championship calendar for
only six seasons, 1999–2004 inclusive. The track was certainly to the
liking of multiple World Champion Valentino Rossi. In 1999, he was
competing in the 250cc World Championship, and won the inaugural
race at Phasika. His first season in 500cc – the last before rebranding
as MotoGP – ended with Rossi becoming World Champion, but he
had to retire after a crash. In the next four years, he won the World
Championship each time with South African MotoGP victories in 2001
and 2004 and runners-up spots in the 2002 and 2003 editions.

☻ ALL-TIME GRAND PRIX WIN LEADERS 1949–2015 ☻

Racer	500	350	250	125	80	50	Total
Giacomo Agostini	68	54	–	–	–	–	122
Valentino Rossi	86	–	14	12	–	–	112
Angel Nieto	–	–	–	62	1	27	90
Mike Hailwood	37	16	21	2	–	–	76
Jorge Lorenzo	40	–	17	4	–	–	61
Mick Doohan	54	–	–	–	–	–	54
Phil Read	11	4	27	10	–	–	52
Dani Pedrosa	28	–	15	8	–	–	51
Marc Marquez	24	–	16	10	–	–	50
Jim Redman	2	21	18	4	–	–	45
Max Biaggi	13	–	29	–	–	–	42
Anton Mang	–	8	33	1	–	–	42
Carlo Ubbiali	–	–	13	26	–	–	39
John Surtees	22	15	1	–	–	–	38
Jorge Martínez	–	–	–	15	22	–	37
Luca Cadalora	8	–	22	4	–	–	34
Geoff Duke	22	11	–	–	–	–	33
Eddie Lawson	31	–	–	–	–	–	31
Kork Ballington	–	14	17	–	–	–	31
Luigi Taveri	–	–	2	22	–	6	30

❀ 1984 500CC FINAL STANDINGS (TOP 10) ❀

Pos	Rider	Nationality	Bike	Pts
1.	Eddie Lawson	(USA)	Yamaha	142
2.	Randy Mamola	(USA)	Honda	111
3.	Raymond Roche	(FRA)	Honda	99
4.	Freddie Spencer	(USA)	Honda	87
5.	Ron Haslam	(GBR)	Honda	77
6.	Barry Sheene	(GBR)	Suzuki	34
7.	Wayne Gardner	(AUS)	Honda	33
8.	Boet van Dulmen	(NED)	Suzuki	25
9.	Didier de Radigues	(BEL)	Chevallier	24
10.	Virginio Ferrari	(ITA)	Yamaha	22

❀ CONSTRUCTORS' FINAL STANDINGS (TOP 5) ❀

Pos	Team	Nationality	Pts
1.	Honda	(JPN)	168
2.	Yamaha	(JPN)	142
3.	Suzuki	(JPN)	64
4.	Chevallier	(FRA)	24
5.	Cagiva	(ITA)	2

❀ NEVER FORGOTTEN ❀

At the end of the 2015 season, a total of 88 riders have died either in racing or in practice for a World Championship race in any of the motorcycle classes. The first fatality was an Englishman, Ben Drinkwater, who lost his life in the 350cc class of the first round of the inaugural F.I.M. World Championship, the Isle of Man TT. On 13 June 1949, Ben was attempting to avoid another competitor when his Norton collided with a bank near Cronk Bane Farm, almost 11 miles into the lap of the Snaefell Mountain Course, and died. The S-bend corner was renamed Drinkwater's Bend in his memory, but it has since reverted to its former name. The most recent racer to die was Italy's 2008 250cc MotoGP World Champion Marco Simoncelli, who died in an accident at the Malaysian MotoGP on 23 October 2011.

Did You Know That?
Victor Surridge from Essex, England, was the first rider to die on the Isle of Man's Snaefell Mountain Course on 27 June 1911. He died in practice in the first year the course hosted a TT race.

❀ HOW MOTOGP'S NEW BOYS FARED IN 2015 ❀

The days with more than 100 men competing in the 500cc World Championship are long gone – 165 men rode in the 1961 season (81 failed to complete a single race and 113 didn't score a point in the 11 races). In 2015 the number of riders on the grid increased from 23 to 25. Colin Edwards – who had retired midway though the season to be replaced by Alex de Angelis – Hiroshi Aoyama, Michael Laverty, and Broc Parkes were off the grid and, as well as de Angelis, the new men were Loris Baz, Eugene Laverty (Michael's younger brother), Marco Melandri, Jack Miller and Maverick Vinales. Four of the riders finished in the top 25 of the final standings, Vinales (12th), Baz (17th), Miller (19th) and Laverty (22nd). De Angelis managed only two points, but Melandri, who had won five MotoGP races in his previous spell between 2003 and 2010, went back to World Superbikes after failing to collect a point in eight races. Both Michael Laverty (20th place) and Parkes (retired) returned for a single race, but Aoyama, however, came back and scored five points

❀ FEDERATION INTERNATIONALE DE CYCLISME ❀

The F.I.M. moved to a new base in 1994, with a permanent staff of only 36. The Board of Directors comprises: President Vito Ippolito (Venezuela), Deputy President Nasser Khalilfa Al Atya (Qatar), Vice-President Andrzej Witkowski (Poland) and a representative from the six CONU (Continental Unions) Presidents. The address is:

11, route Suisse
CH – 1295 Mies
Switzerland

❀ NOT THE SAME WITHOUT UNCLE SAM ❀

Nicky Hayden's decision to leave the MotoGP World Championship at the end of 2015 meant it was likely that the 2016 season would have no riders from the United States for the first time in 40 years.

❀ KAWASAKI'S FIRST WORLD CHAMPION ❀

British racer, Dave Simmonds, won eight of the 11 races in the 1969 125cc World Championship to give Kawasaki their first ever world title. Tragically three years later, on 23 October 1972, just two days before his 33rd birthday, Simmonds died in a fire in his caravan in Rungis, near Paris, after a gas cylinder exploded.

● 1985 500CC FINAL STANDINGS (TOP 10) ●

Pos	Rider	Nationality	Bike	Pts
1.	Freddie Spencer	(USA)	Honda	141
2.	Eddie Lawson	(USA)	Yamaha	133
3.	Christian Sarron	(FRA)	Yamaha	80
4.	Wayne Gardner	(AUS)	Honda	73
=	Ron Haslam	(GBR)	Honda	73
6.	Randy Mamola	(USA)	Honda	72
7.	Raymond Roche	(FRA)	Yamaha	50
8.	Didier de Radigues	(BEL)	Honda	47
9.	Rob McElnea	(GBR)	Suzuki	20
10.	Boet van Dulmen	(NED)	Honda	18
=	Mike Baldwin	(USA)	Honda	18

● CONSTRUCTORS' FINAL STANDINGS (TOP 5) ●

Pos	Team	Nationality	Pts
1.	Honda	(JPN)	168
2.	Yamaha	(JPN)	144
3.	Suzuki	(JPN)	37
4.	Chevallier	(FRA)	3

● FAST TALK (11) ●

"If I'm calling you 'dude' or 'amigo' during the weekend,
it's because I can't remember your name!"
Colin Edwards speaking prior to the
2014 Grand Prix of the Americas

● MOTO2 WORLD CHAMPIONS ●

The Moto2 World Championship replaced the 250cc World Championship in 2010 from the 2010 season. These are the 2010 Moto2 World Championship winners:

Year	Champion	Nationality	Team
2010	Tony Elias	(ESP)	Moriwaki
2011	Stefan Bradl	(GER)	Kalex
2012	Marc Marquez	(ESP)	Suter
2013	Pol Espargaro	(ESP)	Kalex
2014	Esteve Rabat	(ESP)	Kalex
2015	Jogann Zarco	(FRA)	Kalex

❀ SPANISH SIBLING CHAMPIONS ❀

Two out of the three World Champions in 2014 were Spanish racers named Marquez. Older brother Marc (born 17 February 1993) won the MotoGP World Championship for the second time – the youngest rider ever to win two 500cc/MotoGP crowns – while Alex Marquez born 23 April 1996 claimed the Moto3 World Championship.

Did You Know That?
As well as the Espargaro brothers, Pol and Aleix, brothers and rivals in MotoGP, there was another pair of brothers on the grid for the 2015 German MotoGP at the Sachsenring. They were two of the three Laverty brothers from Toomebridge, Northern Ireland, Eugene and Michael, all of whom are motorcycle racers (Jack, the middle brother, competed mainly in British Superbikes).

❀ SWEEPING THE BOARD ❀

The Austrian motorcycle Grand Prix at the Salzburgring circuit on 1 May 1977 was marred by a tragedy in the 350cc race and led to a boycott by 18 of the 32 men who were due to contest the 500cc class. Riders in the 125cc staged a brief sit-in to protest at the state of the track before eventually racing. The winner was Italian Eugenio Lazzarini on a Morbidelli. The 500cc Grand Prix winner was Britain's 42-year-old veteran Jack Findlay on a Suzuki. Five riders failed to finish the 500cc race and all were on Suzuki motorbikes. And, in the 125cc GP, a Morbidelli victory was guaranteed because all 22 bikes on the grid were from that Italian manufacturer.

❀ A PLAYBOY LIFESTYLE ❀

Two-times 500cc World Champion Barry Sheene enjoyed the high life, mixing with the rich and famous from the entertainment and sporting world, including Beatles George Harrison and Ringo Starr, Formula 1 motor-racing World Champion James Hunt, and boxer Henry Cooper. He was invited to participate in many photo shoots and advertisements, often with glamour models, one of whom, Stephanie McLean, became his wife and with whom he had a son and a daughter. Sheene's lifetsyle attracted much interest from the media. One reporter knocked on Barry's front door and said, "I am from the *News of the World*." Barry looked at him, smiled, and replied, "I'm from Putney," before closing the door on the reporter.

❂ 1986 500CC FINAL STANDINGS (TOP 10) ❂

Pos	Rider	Nationality	Bike	Pts
1.	Eddie Lawson	(USA)	Yamaha	139
2.	Wayne Gardner	(AUS)	Honda	117
3.	Randy Mamola	(USA)	Yamaha	105
4.	Mike Baldwin	(USA)	Yamaha	78
5.	Rob McElnea	(GBR)	Yamaha	60
6.	Christian Sarron	(FRA)	Yamaha	58
7.	Didier de Radigues	(BEL)	Honda	42
8.	Raymond Roche	(FRA)	Honda	35
9.	Ron Haslam	(GBR)	Honda	18
10.	Pier-Francesco Chili	(ITA)	Suzuki	11
=	Niall Mackenzie	(GBR)	Suzuki	11

❂ CONSTRUCTORS' FINAL STANDINGS (TOP 5) ❂

Pos	Team	Nationality	Pts
1.	Yamaha	(JPN)	154
2.	Honda	(JPN)	122
3.	Chevallier	(FRA)	42
4.	Suzuki	(JPN)	23
5.	Elf-Honda	(JPN)	14

❂ RECORD-BREAKING SEASON-OPENER ❂

The 2015 MotoGP World Championship season had a record-breaking opening when 36-year-old Valentino Rossi won the Qatar Grand Prix. Only Harold Daniell, aged 39, who won the very first 500cc Motorcycle Grand Prix, the 1949 Isle of Man TT, was older than the Yamaha rider. Rossi was also the oldest leader of the World Championship standings since Jack Findlay, who at 42 years old in 1977 shared top spot with Barry Sheene. Italian riders, with Rossi, Andrea Dovizioso and Andrea Iannone, filled the podium for the first time since Loris Capirossi, Rossi and Marco Melandri finished one-two-three at the 2006 Japan GP.

❂ POSTHUMOUS AWARD FOR SIMONCELLI ❂

On 3 February 2014, the F.I.M. announced that Marco Simoncelli would become the 21st MotoGP Legend. A special ceremony was held at Mugello, Italy, on 30 May as Marco joined compatriots Giacomo Agostini and Carlo Ubbiali on the list of illustrious names.

❂ 125CC/MOTO3 WORLD CHAMPIONS ❂

The 125cc World Championship ran from the inaugural season, 1949, to 2011, after which it was rebranded as Moto3. These men have been 125cc/Moto3 World Champions:

125cc Champions

Year	Champion	Country
1949	Nello Pagani	ITA
1950	Bruno Ruffo	ITA
1951	Carlo Ubbiali	ITA
1952	Cecil Sandford	GBR
1953	Werner Haas	GER
1954	Rupert Hollaus	AUT
1955	Carlo Ubbiali	ITA
1956	Carlo Ubbiali	ITA
1957	Tarquinio Provini	ITA
1958	Carlo Ubbiali	ITA
1959	Carlo Ubbiali	ITA
1960	Carlo Ubbiali	ITA
1961	Tom Phillis	AUS
1962	Luigi Taveri	SWI
1963	Hugh Anderson	NZL
1964	Luigi Taveri	SWI
1965	Hugh Anderson	NZL
1966	Luigi Taveri	SWI
1967	Bill Ivy	GBR
1968	Phil Read	GBR
1969	Dave Simmonds	GBR
1970	Dieter Braun	GER
1971	Angel Nieto	ESP
1972	Angel Nieto	ESP
1973	Kent Andersson	SWE
1974	Kent Andersson	SWE
1975	Paolo Pileri	ITA
1976	Pierpaolo Bianchi	ITA
1977	Pierpaolo Bianchi	ITA
1978	Eugenio Lazzarini	ITA
1979	Angel Nieto	ESP
1980	Pierpaolo Bianchi	ITA
1981	Angel Nieto	ESP
1982	Angel Nieto	ESP
1983	Angel Nieto	ESP

125cc Champions

Year	Champion	Country
1984	Angel Nieto	ESP
1985	Fausto Gresini	ITA
1986	Luca Cadalora	ITA
1987	Fausto Gresini	ITA
1988	Jorge Martinez	ESP
1989	Alex Criville	ESP
1990	Loris Capirossi	ITA
1991	Loris Capirossi	ITA
1992	Alessandro Gramigni	ITA
1993	Dirk Raudies	GER
1994	Kazuto Sakata	JPN
1995	Haruchika Aoki	JPN
1996	Haruchika Aoki	JPN
1997	Valentino Rossi	ITA
1998	Kazuto Sakata	JPN
1999	Emilio Alzamora	ESP
2000	Roberto Locatelli	ITA
2001	Manuel Poggiali	ITA
2002	Arnaud Vincent	FRA
2003	Daniel Pedrosa	ESP
2004	Andrea Dovizioso	ITA
2005	Thomas Luthi	SWI
2006	Alvaro Bautista	ESP
2007	Gabor Talmacsi	HUN
2008	Mike Di Meglio	FRA
2009	Julian Simon	ESP
2010	Marc Marquez	ESP
2011	Nicolas Terol	ESP

Moto3 Champions

Year	Champion	Country
2012	Sandro Cortese	GER
2013	Maverick Vinales	ESP
2014	Alex Marquez	ESP
2015	Danny Kent	GBR

● 1987 500CC FINAL STANDINGS (TOP 10) ●

Pos	Rider	Nationality	Bike	Pts
1.	Wayne Gardner	(AUS)	Honda	178
2.	Randy Mamola	(USA)	Roberts	158
3.	Eddie Lawson	(USA)	Yamaha	157
4.	Ron Haslam	(GBR)	Honda	72
5.	Niall Mackenzie	(GBR)	Honda	61
6.	Tadahiko Taira	(JPN)	Yamaha	56
7.	Christian Sarron	(FRA)	Sonauto	52
8.	Pier-Francesco Chili	(ITA)	Honda	47
9.	Shunji Yatsushiro	(JPN)	Honda	40
10.	Rob McElnea	(GBR)	Yamaha	39

● CONSTRUCTORS' FINAL STANDINGS (TOP 5) ●

Pos	Team	Nationality	Pts
1.	Yamaha	(JPN)	204
2.	Honda	(JPN)	186
3.	Honda/Elf	(JPN)	72
4.	Cagiva	(ITA)	36
5.	Suzuki	(JPN)	31

● TWIN-CYLINDER CHAMPION ●

Leslie Graham was 10 days short of his 38th birthday when he won the inaugural 500cc World Championship. His bike was an AJS 497cc Porcupine, the only two-cylinder machine to win the 500cc title. He won the second and fifth races, the Swiss and Ulster Grands Prix and finished one point ahead of Nello Pagani in the final standings.

Did You Know That?
A pilot, flying Lancaster bombers during World War 2, Graham received a Distinguished Flying Cross before returning to civilian life working for AMC (Associated Motorcycles).

● F.I.M. AFFILIATION ●

The Federation Internationale de Motocyclisme has 112 affiliated members, known as National Motorcycle Federations (FMN), and they are subdivided into six Continental Unions (Africa, Asia, Europe, Latin America, North America and Oceania). Continental Unions are also known as CONUs.

❀ FANTASY 500CC/MOTOGP
UNITED STATES STARTING GRID ❀

(to the end of the 2015 season)

1
Eddie Lawson
*(31 GP wins, 1
World Championship
(1988)*

2
Wayne Rainey
*(24 GP wins, 3
World Championships
1990, 1991, 1992)*

3
Kenny Roberts Sr
*(22 GP wins, 3
World Championships
1978, 1979, 1980)*

4
Freddie Spencer
*(20 GP wins, 2
World Championships
1983, 1985)*

5
Kevin Schwantz
*(5 GP wins, 1 World
Championship 1993)*

6
Randy Mamola
*(13 GP wins, best
2nd, 1980, 1981,
1984, 1987)*

7
Kenny Roberts Jr
*(8 GP wins, 1 World
Championship 2000)*

8
John Kocinski
*(4 GP wins,
best 250cc World
Champion 1990)*

9
Nicky Hayden
*(3 GP wins, 1 World
Championship 2006)*

10
Pat Hennen
*(3 GP wins, best
3rd, 1976, 1977)*

● EDDIE LAWSON – STEADY EDDIE ●

Eddie Lawson was born into a bike-crazy family on 11 March 1958 in California. He was seven years old when he rode an 80cc minibike and competed in dirt-track races near to his Los Angeles home. A dirt-track regular, Eddie achieved AMA Expert status before his 20th birthday in 1978 and finished second behind Freddie Spencer in the 1979 AMA 250cc Road Racing National Championship. Eddie turned professional as a road racer in 1980 and Kawasaki signed him to ride in both AMA Superbike and AMA 250cc Grand Prix Championships.

Riding a Kawasaki for Team Muzzy, Eddie won the 1981 and 1982 AMA Superbike Championship, but his big break came in 1983 when Marlboro Agostini Yamaha signed him to be Kenny Roberts's team-mate and he ended his debut 500cc World Championship season in fourth place. The following season Eddie dominated the 500cc World Championship, winning four times and never being out of the top four on his way to the title. This habit of achieving high finishes earned him the nickname "Steady Eddie".

In 1985, he lost his 500cc crown by eight points to the 1983 World Champion, Freddie Spencer, who doubled up with the 250cc title. Eddie was back in 1986 and won seven GPs on the way to his second 500cc World Championship. Five wins in 1987 was good enough for only third place in the 500cc World Championship behind new top-dog Wayne Gardner and Randy Mamola. Gardner, runner-up in 1986, suffered the same fate in 1998 as Eddie won seven GPs and finished 23 points clear for his third 500cc World Championship. He had already announced that he was moving from Yamaha to their fiercest rivals, Honda, for the 1989 campaign, as Gardner's team-mate. A broken leg scuppered Gardner's 1989 season, but Eddie was pushed all the way by Yamaha's Wayne Rainey. In the end, Eddie became the first rider to be 500cc World Champion in consecutive seasons for two different manufacturers.

Eddie's old team-mate Kenny Roberts persuaded Eddie to ride for Marlboro Roberts Yamaha in 1980, but he could do no better than six podium finishes, no wins and seventh in the 500cc World Championship, with team-mate Rainey winning the first of his three straight world titles. After one season with Roberts, Eddie took up a new challenge, joining Cagiva Corse to help the Italian outfit develop their GP500 machine. In ten years of 500cc racing, Cagiva were still waiting for a top-ten GP finish. Cagiva had contemplated leaving the sport until Eddie agreed to join them. In 1991, Eddie finished in the top eight 11 times in 13 Grands Prix and ended sixth overall in the 500cc World Championship. Then, on 12 July 1992, in round 9 of the

500cc World Championship, the Hungarian GP at the Hungaroring, "Steady Eddie" lived up to his name by delivering Cagiva's first GP win. It was his 31st and final 500c Grand Prix victory. Eddie ended his last 500cc season in ninth place in the World Championship.

Did You Know That?
That 31st victory in the 500cc 1992 Hungarian Grand Prix put Eddie third in the all-time list.

❡ 1988 500CC FINAL STANDINGS (TOP 10) ❡

Pos	Rider	Nationality	Bike	Pts
1.	Eddie Lawson	(USA)	Yamaha	252
2.	Wayne Gardner	(AUS)	Honda	229
3.	Wayne Rainey	(USA)	Yamaha	189
4.	Christian Sarron	(FRA)	Yamaha	149
5.	Kevin Magee	(AUS)	Yamaha	138
6.	Niall Mackenzie	(GBR)	Honda	125
7.	Didier de Radigues	(BEL)	Yamaha	120
8.	Kevin Schwantz	(USA)	Suzuki	119
9.	Pier-Francesco Chili	(ITA)	Honda	110
10.	Rob McElnea	(GBR)	Suzuki	83

❡ CONSTRUCTORS' FINAL STANDINGS (TOP 5) ❡

Pos	Team	Nationality	Pts
1.	Yamaha	(JPN)	280
2.	Honda	(JPN)	242
3.	Suzuki	(JPN)	157
4.	Elf-Honda	(JPN)	68
5.	Cagiva	(ITA)	8

❡ 125CC REDEMPTION FOR NELLO PAGANI ❡

Nello Pagani finished runner-up behind Leslie Graham in the inaugural 500cc World Championship, losing by a single point, only because the best three scores counted and the Italian's two victories and a third place was trumped by the Englishman's win double and a runners-up spot. Switching from a Gilera in the 500cc to a 125cc Mondial, Pagani repeated his two wins, but this time a fifth place in the Nations Grand Prix at Monza, Italy, was enough for him to secure the inaugural 125cc World Championship.

● 1989 500CC FINAL STANDINGS (TOP 10) ●

Pos	Rider	Nationality	Bike	Pts
1.	Eddie Lawson	(USA)	Honda	228
2.	Wayne Rainey	(USA)	Yamaha	210.5
3.	Christian Sarron	(FRA)	Yamaha	165.5
4.	Kevin Schwantz	(USA)	Suzuki	162.5
5.	Kevin Magee	(AUS)	Yamaha	138.5
6.	Pier-Francesco Chili	(ITA)	Honda	122
7.	Niall Mackenzie	(GBR)	Yamaha	103
8.	Ron Haslam	(GBR)	Suzuki	86
9.	Mick Doohan	(AUS)	Honda	81
10.	Wayne Gardner	(AUS)	Honda	67

● CONSTRUCTORS' FINAL STANDINGS (TOP 5) ●

Pos	Team	Nationality	Pts
1.	Honda	(JPN)	257
2.	Yamaha	(JPN)	227.5
3.	Suzuki	(JPN)	211.5
4.	Cagiva	(ITA)	38
5.	Fior	(ITA)	33

● 25 YEARS OF ITALIAN 500CC DOMINATION ●

Italian-built bikes completely dominated motorcycle racing for a quarter of a century. In 24 of the 25 seasons, from 1950–74, either Gilera or MV Agusta won the 500cc Manufacturers' Championship or the rider was 500cc World Champion – often both (British rider Geoff Duke and manufacturer Norton won the titles in 1951). In other classes, Italian constructors Mondial and Moto Guzzi joined the run of success. Gilera claimed six 500cc World Championships in 1950, 1952–55 and 1957 whilst MV Agusta won in 1956, 1958 and 1959. In fact, MV Agusta claimed a World Championship clean sweep of all four categories in 1958, 1959 and 1960. Indeed, an MV Agusta rider was the 500cc World Champion every year from 1958 to 1974 (largely thanks to Giacomo Agostini's nine titles), after which Japanese-manufactured bikes seized control of the sport. MV Agusta (Meccanica Verghera Agusta) was founded on 12 February 1945 near Milan and began as an offshoot of the Agusta Aviation Company which was set up by Count Giovanni Agusta. Meccanica is Italian for mechanics, while Verghera was the name of the small hamlet where the first MV bikes were made.

⚫ GREATEST RACES (7) – 1988 FRENCH GP ⚫

Round 11 of the 1988 season was at Paul Ricard in France, the last time the full-length 5.81km (3.61-mile) circuit was used. Veteran Christian Sarron (Yamaha), pleased the home crowd by taking his fifth consecutive pole – and the last of his career.

On the most famous part of the circuit, the 1.8km Mistral Straight, Wayne Gardner let his Honda use its power and raced into the lead, followed into the Courbe de Signes by Kevin Schwantz (Suzuki), Niall MacKenzie (Honda), Wayne Rainey (Yamaha) and Sarron. The Yamahas and the Suzukis were no match for the pure speed of the Hondas on the straight, but the Honda was weaker going around the corners.

Going into the final lap, Gardner, Lawson, Sarron and Schwantz were battling for the lead. Gardner had a mechanical problem and limped home in fourth. Lawson took the chequered flag, just in front of Sarron, with Schwantz third in one of the closest ever top-three finishes. Sarron was 0.220 seconds behind Lawson and 0.240 seconds ahead of Schwantz, whose reaction to a first podium finish in five races was to do a wheelie passing the finishing line.

1988 French Grand Prix – Circuit Paul Ricard – Sunday 24 July

Pos	Pts	Rider (Nationality)	Bike	Time/Gap
1.	20	Eddie Lawson (USA)	Yamaha	44m 30.727s
2.	17	Christian Sarron (FRA)	Yamaha	+0.220s
3.	15	Kevin Schwantz (USA)	Suzuki	+0.460s
4.	13	Wayne Gardner (AUS)	Honda	+5.720s
5.	11	Wayne Rainey (USA)	Yamaha	+17.630s

Did You Know That?
The partisan home crowd had double reason for optimism on race day. Christian Sarron took pole for the 500cc race, and brother Dominique did likewise for the 250cc race. However, neither won their races: Christian finished second and Dominique third.

⚫ REBEL WITH A CAUSE ⚫

Che Guevara, the Argentine Marxist revolutionary, who became a hero in Cuba, trained to be a doctor. He made a famous motorbike pilgrimage in 1952, riding a famous British 500cc bike, a Norton, and was radicalized by the poverty, hunger, and disease he witnessed on this journey around South America. Guevara called his bike *La Poderosa*, the Powerful.

◉ 1990 500CC FINAL STANDINGS (TOP 10) ◉

Pos	Rider	Nationality	Bike	Pts
1.	Wayne Rainey	(USA)	Yamaha	225
2.	Kevin Schwantz	(USA)	Suzuki	188
3.	Mick Doohan	(AUS)	Honda	179
4.	Niall Mackenzie	(GBR)	Suzuki	140
5.	Wayne Gardner	(AUS)	Honda	138
6.	Juan Garriga	(SPA)	Yamaha	121
7.	Eddie Lawson	(USA)	Yamaha	118
8.	Jean-Philippe Ruggia	(FRA)	Yamaha	110
9.	Christian Sarron	(FRA)	Yamaha	84
10.	Sito Pons	(SPA)	Honda	76

◉ CONSTRUCTORS' FINAL STANDINGS (TOP 5) ◉

Pos	Team	Nationality	Pts
1.	Yamaha	(JPN)	257
2.	Honda	(JPN)	202
3.	Suzuki	(JPN)	197
4.	Cagiva	(ITA)	98
5.	Plaisir	(FRA)	4

◉ FAST TALK (12) ◉

"Riding a race bike is an art – a thing that you do because
you feel something inside."
Valentino Rossi

◉ EUROPEANS RULE THE ROOST ◉

The MotoGP World Championship has been dominated by European
riders for most of the sport's history, but in the past 20 years they have
enjoyed success on Japanese motorcycles. The last time a European
marque won the title, the racer was Casey Stoner from Australia.

◉ CALL HIM PRECOCIOUS ◉

Walter Villa was born in 1943 in Italy. In 1956, aged 13, he rode
in his first race, aboard a 175cc Moto Morini, and finished third,
but behind him was a rider who became one of the greatest of all
time, Giacomo Agostini. Villa himself went on to win four World
Championships, three times in the 250cc class and once in the 350cc.

❂ TRIUMPH WAS A 500CC EXAGGERATION ❂

Triumph Engineering Co. Ltd was a British motorcycle manufacturing company, based in the English Midlands. The company was founded by a German, Siegfried Bettmann, in 1884, as the S. Bettmann & Co. Import Export Agency but he changed the name to Triumph two years later. Triumph competed in the inaugural 500cc World Championship race, the 1949 Isle of Man TT, and New Zealander Syd Jensen finished fifth in the race, good enough to ensure he finished 11th in the final standings. The company raced in many World Championship seasons, but never won a 500cc race.

❂ AN ELITE GROUP IN 2015 ❂

There had never been a more successful grid than the one which started races in the 2015 MotoGP World Championship. Fourteen racers had been crowned World Champion in one class or type of motorcycle racing. In addition seven riders had won a combined 169 500cc/MotoGP races and 19 men could boast 390 Grands Prix victories in all classes. This is the honour roll of World Champions:

Rider	Country	No.	Title/s (Year/s)
Valentino Rossi	ITA	9	125cc (1997)
			250cc (1999)
			500cc/MotoGP (2001, 2002, 2003, 2004, 2005, 2008, 2009)
Jorge Lorenzo	ESP	4	250cc (2006, 2007)
			MotoGP (2010, 2012)
Marc Marquez	ESP	4	125cc (2010)
			Moto2 (2012
			MotoGP (2013, 2014)
Dani Pedrosa	ESP	3	125cc (2003)
			250cc (2004, 2005)
Hiroshi Aoyama	JPN	1	250cc (2009)
Alvaro Bautista	ESP	1	125cc (2006)
Stefan Bradl	GER	1	Moto2 (2011)
Cal Crutchlow	GBR	1	Supersport (2009)
Andrea Dovizioso	ITA	1	125cc (2004)
Tony Elias	ESP	1	Moto2 (2010)
Pol Espargaro	ESP	1	Moto2 (2013)
Nicky Hayden	USA	1	MotoGP (2006)
Marco Melandri	ITA	1	250cc (2002)
Maverick Vinales	ESP	1	Moto3 (2013)

❀ 1991 500CC FINAL STANDINGS (TOP 10) ❀

Pos	Rider	Nationality	Bike	Pts
1.	Wayne Rainey	(USA)	Yamaha	233
2.	Mick Doohan	(AUS)	Honda	224
3.	Kevin Schwantz	(USA)	Suzuki	204
4.	John Kocinski	(USA)	Yamaha	161
=	Wayne Gardner	(AUS)	Honda	161
6.	Eddie Lawson	(USA)	Cagiva	126
7.	Juan Garriga	(SPA)	Yamaha	121
8.	Didier de Radigues	(BEL)	Suzuki	105
9.	Doug Chandler	(USA)	Yamaha	85
10.	Jean-Philippe Ruggia	(FRA)	Yamaha	78

❀ CONSTRUCTORS' FINAL STANDINGS (TOP 5) ❀

Pos	Team	Nationality	Pts
1.	Yamaha	(JPN)	252
2.	Honda	(JPN)	239
3.	Suzuki	(JPN)	205
4.	Cagiva	(ITA)	100
5.	Suzuki/Yamaha	(JPN)	19

❀ MY NAME'S ON IT ❀

Walter Villa entered his first race in 1956, started his international racing career only in 1967 – with the Spanish marque Montesa – and retired in 1980 with Harley Davidson (he did not compete in 1968 and 1971). In 1968, Walter and his brother, Francesco – who had previously designed two-stroke bikes for Mondial and Montesa – began designing and building their own motorcycles at their home near Modena, Italy. A year later, Walter entered the 125cc F.I.M. Motorcycle World Road Racing Championship, riding either a Montesa or a Villa, and the 250cc class exclusively on a Villa. Walter finished only twice during that 1969 season: third in the 125cc Spanish Grand Prix and fourth in the 125cc Nations Grand Prix on a Villa. Walter raced a Villa for the last time in the 1970 125cc Spanish Grand Prix and then raced for Yamaha, Kawasaki, Benelli and Harley Davidson. Harley Davidson signed Walter for the 1974 season following the death of Renzo Pasolini at Monza in May 1973. He enjoyed tremendous success riding the Harley Davidson, winning three consecutive 250cc World Championships, 1974–76, and in 1976 he also took the 350cc class for the famous American marque.

❂ 500CC/MOTOGP BRITISH GP WINNERS 1977–2015 ❂

Year	Rider	Nat	Bike
1977*	Pat Hennen	USA	Suzuki
1978*	Kenny Roberts	USA	Yamaha
1979*	Kenny Roberts	USA	Yamaha
1980*	Randy Manola	USA	Suzuki
1981*	Jack Middelburg	USA	Suzuki
1982*	Franco Uncini	ITA	Suzuki
1983*	Kenny Roberts	USA	Yamaha
1984*	Randy Mamola	USA	Honda
1985*	Freddie Spencer	USA	Honda
1986†	Wayne Gardner	AUS	Honda
1987†	Eddie Lawson	USA	Yamaha
1988†	Wayne Rainey	USA	Yamaha
1989†	Kevin Schwantz	USA	Suzuki
1990†	Kevin Schwantz	USA	Suzuki
1991†	Kevin Schwantz	USA	Suzuki
1992†	Wayne Gardner	AUS	Honda
1993†	Luca Cadalora	ITA	Yamaha
1994†	Kevin Schwantz	USA	Suzuki
1995†	Mick Doohan	AUS	Honda
1996†	Mick Doohan	AUS	Honda
1997†	Mick Doohan	AUS	Honda
1998†	Simon Crafar	AUS	Yamaha
1999†	Alex Creville	SPA	Honda
2000†	Valentino Rossi	ITA	Honda
2001†	Valentino Rossi	ITA	Honda
2002†	Valentino Rossi	ITA	Honda
2003†	Max Biaggi	ITA	Honda
2004†	Valentino Rossi	ITA	Yamaha
2005†	Valentino Rossi	ITA	Yamaha
2006†	Dani Pedrosa	SPA	Honda
2007†	Casey Stoner	AUS	Ducati
2008†	Casey Stoner	AUS	Ducati
2009†	Andrea Dovizioso	ITA	Honda
2010*	Jorge Lorenzo	SPA	Yamaha
2011*	Casey Stoner	AUS	Honda
2012*	Jorge Lorenzo	SPA	Yamaha
2013*	Jorge Lorenzo	SPA	Yamaha
2014*	Marc Marquez	SPA	Honda
2015*	Valentino Rossi	ITA	Yamaha

* = at Silverstone; † = at Donington Park

✹ 1992 500CC FINAL STANDINGS (TOP 10) ✹

Pos	Rider	Nationality	Bike	Pts
1.	Wayne Rainey	(USA)	Yamaha	140
2.	Mick Doohan	(AUS)	Honda	136
3.	John Kocinski	(USA)	Yamaha	102
4.	Kevin Schwantz	(USA)	Suzuki	99
5.	Doug Chandler	(USA)	Suzuki	94
6.	Wayne Gardner	(AUS)	Honda	78
7.	Juan Garriga	(SPA)	Yamaha	61
8.	Alex Criville	(SPA)	Honda	59
9.	Eddie Lawson	(USA)	Cagiva	56
10.	Randy Mamola	(USA)	Yamaha	45

✹ CONSTRUCTORS' FINAL STANDINGS (TOP 4) ✹

Pos	Team	Nationality	Pts
1.	Honda	(JPN)	186
2.	Yamaha	(JPN)	168
3.	Suzuki	(JPN)	127
4.	Cagiva	(ITA)	69

✹ FIRST TO 50 ✹

Japanese giants Honda began racing in the Motorcycle World Championship in 1966, making them – in 2015 – the first marque to reach 50 seasons.

✹ GERMAN KING ✹

Dieter Konig made his reputation as an engine manufacturer and as a hydroplane racer. His engines powered motorcycles in most of the World Championship classes before they formed their own team. In 1973, two Konig racers finished in the top 10 in the final 500cc World Championship standings, with New Zealander Kim Newcombe, runner-up – Dieter Hiller was eighth – also claiming the first 500cc victory for the team in the Yugoslavia Grand Prix at Opatija.

✹ FROM RACER TO TEAM OWNER ✹

When Takazumi Katayama, Japan's first World Champion – he won the 1977 350cc title – retired from racing he became a Motorcycle Grand Prix Team owner, Katayama-Honda.

❂ FAST OFF THE MARC ❂

The highest top speed currently recorded in MotoGP is 217.66mph (349.23kmh) set by Spain's Marc Marquez on a Honda RC213V in the 2015 German Grand Prix at the Sachsenring. By comparison the fastest speed achieved in Formula One is 231.52mph (372.6kmh), set by Colombian driver, Juan Pablo Montoya, driving a McLaren Mercedes at the 2005 Italian Grand Prix.

❂ TWO HEADS BETTER THAN ONE ❂

The inaugural World Championship season, 1949, included a sidecar championship. For the first two years, the sidecar World Championship used 600cc bikes. The first World Champions were the British pair of Eric Oliver and Denis Jenkinson with Norton machinery. The following season, the title went to British rider Eric Oliver and his Italian passenger, Lorenzo Dobelli. When the 1951 Sidecar World Championship switched to 500cc motorcycles, the defending champions retained the title.

❂ CLOSE BUT NO CIGAR FOR RANDY ❂

Randy Mamola, born in San Jose, California, on 10 November 1959, is recognized as one of the greatest riders never to be a 500cc World Champion. In ten seasons between 1979 and 1988, riding for Yamaha (two spells), Suzuki, Honda and Cagiva, he enjoyed at least one podium finish. Mamola won 13 races, with the best in any season being three, in 1984 for Honda and in 1987, his second Yamaha stint. In both years, he finished runner-up in the 500cc World Championship, beaten by Eddie Lawson in 1984 and Wayne Gardner in 1987. Earlier, in both 1980 and 1981, with Suzuki, Kenny Roberts and Marco Lucchinelli, respectively, beat Mamola to the title, making a total of four runners-up finishes.

❂ BELGIAN GP BOYCOTT OVER SAFETY ❂

The 1979 Belgian Motorcycle Grand Prix at Spa-Francorchamps was boycotted by top riders because they were unhappy with safety at the famous circuit and the way the F.I.M. ran the Motorcycle World Championship. The same riders also threatened to set up a rival organization – provisionally called the World Series – and this had an almost immediate effect. The governing body amended the way races were controlled, improved safety procedures and there was also an increase in prize money.

❂ FANTASY 500CC/MOTOGP
AUSTRALIAN STARTING GRID ❂

(to the end of the 2015 season)

1
Mick Doohan
(54 GP wins, 5
World Championships
1994, 1995, 1996,
1997, 1998)

2
Casey Stoner
(38 GP wins, 2
World Championships
2007, 2011)

3
Wayne Gardner
(18 GP wins, 1
World Championship
1987)

4
Daryl Beattie
(3 GP wins, best
2nd, 1995)

5
Jack Findlay
(3 GP wins, best 2nd,
1968)

6
Garry McCoy
(3 GP wins, best
5th, 2000)

7
Jack Ahearn
(1 GP win, best 2nd,
1964)

8
Kevin Magee
(1 GP win, best 5th,
1988, 1989)

9
Troy Bayliss
(1 GP win, Superbike
World Champion
2001, 2006, 2008)

10
Chris Vermeulen
(1 GP win, best 6th,
2007)

❦ FAST TALK (13) ❦

"Death is not evil, for it frees man from all ills and takes away his desires along with desire's rewards. Old age is the supreme evil, for it deprives man of all pleasures while allowing his appetites to remain, and it brings with it every possible sorrow.
Yet men fear death and desire old age."
Giacomo Agostini

❦ CONSTRUCTORS' WORLD CHAMPIONSHIPS ❦

Constructor	Country	Total	First	Most Recent
Honda	JPN	21	1983	2014
MV Agusta	ITA	18	1956	1974
Yamaha	JPN	17	1975	2015
Gilera	ITA	6	1950	1957
Suzuki	JPN	6	1976	2000
AJS	GBR	1	1949	1949
Norton	GBR	1	1951	1951
Ducati	ITA	1	2007	2007

❦ THE FIRST 350CC KINGS ❦

Birmingham motorcycle manufacturer Veloce was founded by John Goodman in 1904. A small, family-owned company they were unlike the larger factories in the English Midlands, in that they concentrated on hand-built machines. Their first two-stroke motorbike was called the Velocette and that became the name of all their bikes. Velocette had limited success in the first 500cc World Championship, but they dominated the 350cc class. Freddie Frith won all five races and became the inaugural 350cc World Champion. The following season, Bob Foster finished top of the standings in the same class to give Velocette their second last World Championship.

Did You Know That?
Velocette had five riders in the 1949 350cc World Championship top 10: Frith, Foster, David Whitworth, Ernie Lyons and Charlie Salt.

❦ UBIALLI IS ALMOST PERFECT – TWICE ❦

Italy's Carlo Ubialli was the 1956 125cc and 250cc World Champion, winning five of six races in both classes. Compatriot Romolo Ferri won the 125cc German Grand Prix and Swiss ace Luigi Taveri took the Ulster GP.

❀ MICK DOOHAN – THE WIZARD OF OZ ❀

Michael "Mick" Sydney Doohan was born on 4 June 1965 on Queensland's Gold Coast in eastern Australia. He began his racing career in Australian Superbikes and made his international debut – riding for Yahama – in Japan during the inaugural F.I.M. Superbike World Championship in August 1988. He was unclassified in the first race, but won race two. Round 8 of the Championship was in Sydney and he thrilled the home crowd by not only claiming pole position and setting the fastest lap in the second race, but he won both races, too. Honda persuaded him to jump to the 500cc circuit for the 1999 World Championship, where he was a team-mate of compatriot and 1987 500cc World Champion, Wayne Gardner. Fans loved Mick's racing style, with his lower body close to the track as he cornered. His rookie season displayed promise as he finished third in the German GP, and was ninth in the 50cc World Championship, one place better than Gardner.

Mick won his first 500cc GP in 1990, in Hungary, and finished third in the 500cc World Championship that year. He continued to improve over the next couple of years, achieving a runners-up position in the 1991 500cc World Championship, nine points behind Yamaha's Wayne Rainey, and only four points adrift the following season, having been almost unbeatable at the start of the campaign with four wins and two seconds in the first six races. Sadly, a terrible accident during practice at Assen for the Dutch TT injured his right leg so badly there were fears he would have to have it amputated. His leg was saved, but the injury meant he missed the races in the Netherlands, Hungary, France and Great Britain, which allowed Rainey to claim a third consecutive 500cc World Championship. Unsurprizangly, Mick eased his way back into racing in 1993. His leg took time to heal – as his right foot was still too weak to break, he switched from a foot brake to a left thumb-operated rear brake. Nonetheless he won the 1993 San Marino 500cc GP and was fourth in the World Championship.

Between 1994 and 1997, Mick was at his very best. He gave frequent masterclasses in 500cc racing, winning nine GPs and taking podium finishes in the other six races. His World Championship winning margin was a mammoth 143 points. Mick successfully defended his title in 1995, recording seven victories and three podium finishes. In 1996, the battle seemed to be only for runners-up in the World Championship, because Mick took his third straight title, 64 points clear of his Spanish team-mate Alex Criville. Mick's 143-point World Championship-winning margin of 1994 was repeated in 1997, and he broke Giacomo Agostini's record of GP wins in a season with

12. He was pushed hard in the 1998 season by rookie sensation Max Biaggi – the 250cc World Champion – but won his fifth consecutive title. Sadly, Mick was forced to retire at the age of just 34 years old after suffering yet more multiple leg fractures in qualifying for the 1999 500cc Spanish GP at Jerez.

Did You Know That?
Only Giacomo Agostini – eight – and Valentino Rossi – seven – have won more 500cc/MotoGP World Championship titles than Mick Doohan (five).

❂ 1993 500CC FINAL STANDINGS (TOP 10) ❂

Pos	Rider	Nationality	Bike	Pts
1.	Kevin Schwantz	(USA)	Suzuki	248
2.	Wayne Rainey	(USA)	Yamaha	214
3.	Daryl Beattie	(AUS)	Honda	176
4.	Mick Doohan	(AUS)	Honda	156
5.	Luca Cadalora	(ITA)	Yamaha	145
6.	Alex Barros	(BRA)	Suzuki	125
7.	Shinichi Itoh	(JPN)	Honda	119
8.	Alex Criville	(SPA)	Honda	117
9.	Niall Mackenzie	(GBR)	Yamaha	103
10.	Doug Chandler	(USA)	Cagiva	83

❂ CONSTRUCTORS' FINAL STANDINGS (TOP 4) ❂

Pos	Team	Nationality	Pts
1.	Yamaha	(JPN)	281
2.	Suzuki	(JPN)	259
3.	Cagiva	(ITA)	234
4.	Honda	(JPN)	231

❂ LOTS FOR HOME FANS TO CHEER ❂

The first race in the MotoGP era was on 7 April 2002, the Japanese Grand Prix at Suzuka. Valentino Rossi, the 2001 500cc World Champion, made a perfect start to his title defence, winning by 1.55 seconds from Akira Ryo. The home fans had much more to cheer than Ryo on the podium because five other Japanese riders finished in the first 11: Sinicho Ito (fourth), Norfumi Abe (fifth), Nobuatso Aoki (seventh), Daijiro Kato (10th) and Tetsuya Harada (11th).

❂ 1994 500CC FINAL STANDINGS (TOP 10) ❂

Pos	Rider	Nationality	Bike	Pts
1.	Mick Doohan	(AUS)	Honda	317
2.	Luca Cadalora	(ITA)	Yamaha	174
3.	John Kocinski	(USA)	Cagiva	172
4.	Kevin Schwantz	(USA)	Suzuki	169
5.	Alberto Puig	(SPA)	Honda	152
6.	Alex Criville	(SPA)	Honda	144
7.	Shinichi Itoh	(JPN)	Honda	141
8.	Alex Barros	(BRA)	Suzuki	134
9.	Doug Chandler	(USA)	Cagiva	96
10.	Niall Mackenzie	(GBR)	Yamaha	69

❂ CONSTRUCTORS' FINAL STANDINGS (TOP 5) ❂

Pos	Team	Nationality	Pts
1.	Honda	(JPN)	317
2.	Yamaha	(JPN)	207
3.	Suzuki	(JPN)	199
4.	Cagiva	(ITA)	178
5.	Yamaha/Suzuki	(JPN)	36

❂ BOY RACER ❂

The youngest racer on the grid for the 2015 MotoGP season was Australian Jack Miller. On the opening day of the season, at the Qatar Grand Prix, he was aged 20 years and 70 days. Riding a Honda, he retired in the first race and failed to break into the top 10 in any race during the season.

Did You Know That?
Valentino Rossi was the "old man" of the grid, 15 years and 336 days older than Miller, and the Italian ace went on to win the season-opener riding a Honda.

❂ KNOWING THEIR WAY TO FIRST PLACE ❂

The 2015 MotoGP grid contained winners of more World Championships and Grand Prix races than in any other season. It was a similar story in Moto2, with four former 125cc or Moto3 World Champions on the grid and no fewer than 14 riders having won a combined 83 races between them.

❀ BORN OUT OF DESIRE ❀

The first Italian constructor to win the 500cc World Championship was Gilera, who won four times, in 1952, 1953, 1955 and 1957. Their riders enjoyed even more success, winning six titles, Umberto Masetti in 1950 and 1952, Geoff Duke in 1953, 1954 and 1955 and Libero Liberatti in 1956. The company, whose motto is "Born out of desire", had been founded by Giuseppe Gilera in Arcore in 1909. Gilera moved into racing before World War 2, once they had acquired the rights to use four-cyclinder Rondine engines, and Dorino Serafini won the 1939 European Championship for Gilera. Despite being the team to beat in 500cc racing, Gilera – along with Mondial and Moto Guzzi – decided to pull out of the Motorcycling World Championship, citing the costs and, although it went unsaid, the fact that car sales were booming. Gilera returned to the 500cc World Championship in 1963 and two of their racers, both British, John Hartle and Phil Read, claimed third and fourth places in the final standings. It was a one-year wonder and they weren't competitive again and, in 1969, Gilera was purchased by Piaggio, though the name survived. The racing team returned in the early 2000s and Manuel Poggiali won the 125cc World Championship. Marco Simoncelli brought even greater success later in the decade, winning the 2008 250cc World Championship and finishing third the following year.

❀ WORLD CHAMPIONS IN IOM TT RANKINGS ❀

The Isle of Man Tourist Trophy series pre-dates the Motorcycle World Championship by more than 40 years, and the Senior race was part of the 500cc World Championship calendar from 1949 to 1976. None of the World Champions can match the Isle of Man records of Joey Dunlop, who won 26 races, or the present-day King of the Isle of Man, John McGuinness, 21 wins. Third on the rankings, with 17 race wins, is Dave Molyneaux. However, there are half a dozen World Champions who are on the honours board with more than one victory on the daunting Snaefell Mountain Course:

IOM rank	Racer	IOM wins
4	Mike Hailwood	14
6	Giacomo Agostini	10
8	Phil Read	8
10	Geoff Duke	6
10	John Surtees	6
14	Gary Hocking	2

⚙ 1995 500CC FINAL STANDINGS (TOP 10) ⚙

Pos	Rider	Nationality	Bike	Pts
1.	Mick Doohan	(AUS)	Honda	248
2.	Daryl Beattie	(AUS)	Suzuki	215
3.	Luca Cadalora	(ITA)	Yamaha	176
4.	Alex Criville	(SPA)	Honda	166
5.	Shinichi Ito	(JPN)	Honda	127
6.	Loris Capirossi	(ITA)	Honda	108
7.	Alex Barros	(BRA)	Honda	104
8.	Alberto Puig	(SPA)	Honda	99
9.	Norifumi Abe	(JPN)	Yamaha	81
10.	Loris Reggiani	(ITA)	Aprilia	59

⚙ CONSTRUCTORS' FINAL STANDINGS (TOP 5) ⚙

Pos	Team	Nationality	Pts
1.	Honda	(JPN)	301
2.	Suzuki	(JPN)	205
3.	Yamaha	(JPN)	177
4.	Aprilia	(ITA)	59
5.	Cagiva	(JPN)	6

⚙ FAST TALK (14) ⚙

"If Valentino Rossi won a race for Ducati, it would be like
the Pope winning at Monza in a Ferrari."
*Journalist and commentator Toby Moody is excited at the thought
of Rossi riding for an Italian team in 2011. Rossi had only
three podium finishes – but no wins– in two years.*

⚙ MIKE THE BIKE HAS A BUSY SEASON ⚙

Mike Hailwood is considered one of the all-time greats of the
Motorcycle World Championship, winning a total of nine titles. He
also won exactly half of his 152 starts, peaking in 1966, his first
year with Honda in the 350cc and 500cc classes. In all, Hailwood
picked up one point from his only outing in 125cc, but won an
astonishing 19 races in the other three divisions. Hailwood won ten
times in 250cc, had six victories in 350cc and took three chequered
flags in 500cc. He topped the final standings in both 250cc and
350cc World Championships but, hampered by five retirements, was
beaten into second place for the 500cc title by Giacomo Agostini.

⚫ GREATEST RACES (8) – 1983 SWEDISH GP ⚫

Freddie Spencer (Honda) and Kenny Roberts (Yamaha) had split the first 10 races of the 1983 500cc World Championship, both winning five times, and the former held a two-point lead in the World Championship. At Anderstorp, in the Swedish Grand Prix, their rivalry produced a magnificent race, with a controversial ending.

Roberts's two-stroke V4 Yamaha YZR500 was more powerful than Spencer's two-stroke V3 Honda NS500, and he led Spencer going into the final lap. The pair screamed their way down the back straight where, at the penultimate corner, a 90-degree right-hander, they hit the brakes simultaneously, but Spencer emerged from Roberts's slipstream and got on the inside of the Yamaha.

However, as they exited the corner, they ran wide, off the track and into the dirt. Spencer returned to the tarmac before Roberts, hit the power and beat him by 0.160 seconds. Takazumi Katayama (Honda) finished third, but was bemused to see Roberts and Spencer exchange angry words on the podium. Their dispute has raged for more than 30 years, Spencer calling it a calculated risk, Roberts a dangerous manoeuvre. Whatever the argument, Spencer became the 1983 500cc World Champion.

1983 Swedish Grand Prix – Anderstorp – Sunday 6 August

Pos	Pts	Rider (Nationality)	Bike	Time/Gap
1.	15	Freddie Spencer (USA)	Honda	49m 17.530s
2.	12	Kenny Roberts (Sr) (USA)	Yamaha	+0.160s
3.	10	Takazumi Katayama (JPN)	Honda	+34.700s
4.	8	Marc Fontan (FRA)	Yamaha	+38.220s
5.	6	Eddie Lawson (USA)	Yamaha	+58.500s

Did You Know That?
The Scandinavian Raceway at Anderstorp was built on marshlands in 1968. The longest straight, Flight Straight, was also a 980m (896.8yd/2,688ft) aircraft runway.

⚫ OLDEST 500CC RACE-WINNER ⚫

The oldest ever winner of a 500cc/MotoGP race was Scotsman Fergus Anderson, who rode a Moto Guzzi to victory in the 1953 season-ending Spanish Grand Prix at Barcelona's Montjuich Circuit. Born on 9 February 1909, he was 44 years and 227 days old when he won the race in Spain, his only one in 500cc that season. However, Anderson also won three times in the 350cc class and ended as World Champion.

⚙ 1996 500CC FINAL STANDINGS (TOP 10) ⚙

Pos	Rider	Nationality	Bike	Pts
1.	Mick Doohan	(AUS)	Honda	309
2.	Alex Criville	(SPA)	Honda	245
3.	Luca Cadalora	(ITA)	Honda	168
4.	Alex Barros	(BRA)	Honda	158
5.	Norifumi Abe	(JPN)	Yamaha	148
6.	Scott Russell	(USA)	Suzuki	133
7.	Tadayuki Okada	(JPN)	Honda	132
8.	Carlos Checa	(SPA)	Honda	124
9.	Jean-Michel Bayle	(FRA)	Yamaha	110
10.	Loris Capirossi	(ITA)	Yamaha	98

⚙ CONSTRUCTORS' FINAL STANDINGS (TOP 5) ⚙

Pos	Team	Nationality	Pts
1.	Honda	(JPN)	315
2.	Yamaha	(JPN)	195
3.	Suzuki	(JPN)	181
4.	ELF500	(SUI)	30
5.	Aprilia	(ITA)	24

⚙ RACING BIKES IN THE MOVIES ⚙

A number of marques have provided Motorcycle Grand Prix machines in movies and TV shows. Here are some famous ones:

In *The Great Escape*, the famous wartime film of 1963, Virgil Hilts, played by Steve McQueen, attempts to escape, by jumping a barbed wire border into Switzerland. In reality it wasn't quite the way it was. Insurers refused to allow heart-throb McQueen to do the stunt on a Triumph TR6 and top stuntman Bud Ekins was on the bike in the scene. McQueen was, nonetheless, involved because he was one of the Nazi motorcyclists chasing Hilts. Triumph also provided bikes in *Mission Impossible 2*, with Tom Cruise, playing Ethan Hunt, on a Speed Triple, being chased by a baddie on a Sprint.

In the 1977–83 American television series *CHiPS*, about a pair of highway cops – played by Erik Estrada and Larry Wilcox – they rode Kawasaki Z1000s, with BMW fairings. But Estrada did not have a motorcycle licence, until he passed, at the third attempt, whilst preparing for a later reality TV series.

There have also been a few motorcycle racing biopics. One such was of New Zealander Kim Newcombe, *Love, Speed & Loss*, in 2005.

❀ THE FLEMISH STAR ❀

Didier De Radigues, born in Leuven, Belgium, on 27 March 1958, made his World Championship debut in the 1980 250cc Dutch TT at Assen. His breakthrough year was in 1982, when he collected three of his four career victories, the 350cc Nations Grand Prix and Czechoslovakia GP, and the 250cc Yugoslavia GP. He also finished on the podium in his home race, the 250cc Belgian GP at Spa-Francorchamps, beaten only by German's Anton Mang. In 1983, De Radigues stepped up to race occasionally in 500cc, but also rode in all 11 Grands Prix in 250cc, winning the Belgian Grand Prix and taking three other podiums. De Radigues had limited success in the 500cc World Championship between 1984 and 1988, his best results being third place in both the 1986 British GP and 1988 Austrian GP. In 1990, he took his final podium position, the 250cc Belgian Grand Prix, and it would 23 years before another Belgian, Xavier Simeon, made it to the podium, Simeon finishing third in the 2013 French Moto2. The 1991 500cc season was not only the most consistent of De Radigues's 12-year career, scoring points in 14 out of 15 races, but also his last. The following year, at the request of the riders, he helped form the International Motorcycle Riders Association which was then managed by Franco Uncini at the International Road Racing Teams Association (IRTA). In 1998, he competed in the 24 Hours of Le Mans with a former rival as one of his co-drivers: 1987 500cc World Champion Wayne Gardner.

Did You Know That?
Simeon became only the third Belgian rider to win a Motorcycle Grand Prix when he won the 2015 Moto2 German GP. De Radigues had enjoyed four victories and Julien Vanzeebroeck won three 50cc races in the mid-1970s.

❀ TWO RACES, TWO PODIUM FINISHES ❀

Dick Creith from Bushmills, County Antrim, Northern Ireland, only ever raced in two 500cc Grand Prix races, the 1964 and 1965 Ulster Grand Prix at Dundrod. His first race ended with him riding his Norton into second place, eight seconds behind another Norton, this one ridden by Phil Read. Creith would not be denied in 1965 as he finished 8.8 seconds ahead of South Africa's Paddy Driver on a Matchlesss, with another Norton rider taking third place, Chris Conn. The eight points from winning the Ulster GP was good enough to put Creith in sixth place in the 1965 500cc World Championship final standings.

⬡ 1997 500CC FINAL STANDINGS (TOP 10) ⬡

Pos	Rider	Nationality	Bike	Pts
1.	Mick Doohan	(AUS)	Honda	340
2.	Tadayuki Okada	(JPN)	Honda	197
3.	Nobuatsu Aoki	(JPN)	Honda	179
4.	Alex Criville	(SPA)	Honda	172
5.	Takuma Aoki	(JPN)	Honda	134
6.	Luca Cadalora	(ITA)	Yamaha	129
7.	Norifumi Abe	(JPN)	Yamaha	126
8.	Carlos Checa	(SPA)	Honda	119
9.	Alex Barros	(BRA)	Honda	101
10.	Doriano Romboni	(ITA)	Aprilia	88

⬡ CONSTRUCTORS' FINAL STANDINGS (TOP 5) ⬡

Pos	Team	Nationality	Pts
1.	Honda	(JPN)	375
2.	Yamaha	(JPN)	188
3.	Suzuki	(JPN)	90
4.	Aprilia	(ITA)	88
5.	Mondenas	(MAS)	68

⬡ BREAKING HONDA'S BRITISH MONOPOLY ⬡

New Zealander Simon Crafar, the 1991 Malaysia Superbike Champion, only ever claimed one victory during his motorcycle racing career, winning the 1998 500cc British Grand Prix at Donington Park on a Yamaha. It was not only the last victory on Dunlop tyres in a dry race but also the only non-Honda victory in the 14-race calendar. The other wins went to Mick Doohan, eight, Max Biagi and Alex Criville, two each, and Carlos Checa won the Madrid Grand Prix. In his career, Crafar competed in 32 Grands Prix (26 in 500cc in 1993, 1998 and 1999, and six in 250cc in 1993), taking three podium places, all in 1998 when he finished seventh in the 500cc World Championship standings.

⬡ YOUNG STAR IMPRESSES FUTURE SUPERSTAR ⬡

In 1993, the final year of the category, Norifumi Abe won the 500cc All Japan Road Race Championship becoming, at 17, its youngest ever title-holder. A 14-year-old Valentino Rossi was so impressed with Abe's skilful bike-handling that he nicknamed himself "Rossifumi".

❀ SIMPLY THE BEST ❀

When Kevin Schwantz took the chequered flag on his Suzuki to win the season-ending 500cc Brazilian Grand Prix at the Goiânia Circuit (later renamed Autodromo Internacional Ayrton Senna) on 17 September 1989, Tina Turner was riding high in the worldwide music charts with her single "(Simply) the Best". Texan Schwantz had a frustrating season as he only recorded three types of result in the 15-race campaign: six victories (two more than World Champion Eddie Lawson), three second-places and six retirements. It meant he finished fourth in the 500cc World Championship table.

❀ ARGENTINA'S LAST HOME WINNER ❀

The Autodromo Municipal Ciudad de Buenos Aires hosted the first Argentina Grand Prix. In 1960, it was not part of the World Championship calendar and home rider Juan Carlos Salatini took the victory on a Gilera. The F.I.M. added the Argentina Grand Prix to the 1961 World Championship calendar and there was another home success, this time Jorge Kissling on a Matchless. Benedicto Caldarella rode in the 250cc race that year, but was unclassified. A year later, also riding for Matchless, he was on the top step of the podium after winning the 1962 500cc Argentina Grand Prix. It was his only World Championship race victory and also the last time a home racer won the Argentina GP. Caldarella finished fifth in the 1962 World Championship, rode to third place in both the 250cc and 500cc Argentina GP in 1963 and secured second place in his final Grand Prix outing, the season-ending 1964 Nations Grand Prix at Monza.

❀ 500CC/MOTOGP CHAMPIONS BY COUNTRY ❀

Riders from only six nations have been World Champion in the elite class. Italy boasts not only the most Championships but also the two most prolific winners in the sport's history. This is the full list:

Country	Wins	Racers	First win	Most recent
Italy	20	6	Umberto Masetti 1950	Valentino Rossi 2009
Great Britain	17	6	Leslie Graham 1949	Barry Sheene 1977
United States	15	7	Kenny Roberts 1978	Nicky Hayden 2006
Australia	8	3	Wayne Gardner 1987	Casey Stoner 2011
Spain	6	3	Alex Criville 1999	Jorge Lorenzo 2015
Rhodesia	1	1	Gary Hocking 1961	Gary Hocking 1961

❀ 1998 500CC FINAL STANDINGS (TOP 10) ❀

Pos	Rider	Nationality	Bike	Pts
1.	Mick Doohan	(AUS)	Honda	260
2.	Max Biaggi	(ITA)	Honda	208
3.	Alex Criville	(SPA)	Honda	198
4.	Carlos Checa	(SPA)	Honda	139
5.	Alex Barros	(BRA)	Honda	138
6.	Norick Abe	(JPN)	Yamaha	128
7.	Simon Crafer	(NZL)	Yamaha	119
8.	Tadayuki Okada	(JPN)	Honda	106
9.	Nobuatsu Aoki	(JPN)	Suzuki	101
10.	Regis Laconi	(FRA)	Yamaha	86

❀ CONSTRUCTORS' FINAL STANDINGS (TOP 5) ❀

Pos	Team	Nationality	Pts
1.	Honda	(JPN)	345
2.	Yamaha	(JPN)	186
3.	Suzuki	(JPN)	84
4.	Modenas	(MAS)	65
5.	Muz	(GER)	11

❀ THE PAPA ❀

Italy's Marco Papa, born on 16 March 1958, spent 16 years in Grand Prix Motorcycle Racing, 1980–96, and enjoyed his best ever season in 1990 when, riding a Honda, he finished in 13th position in the 500cc World Championship. Sadly Papa didn't have a chance to enjoy a long retirement as he died in a road traffic accident on 9 September 1999 near Adro, Italy. A turn was dedicated to him at the Magione Circuit near his Perugia birthplace.

Did You Know That?
Marco Papa's last 500cc World Championship point came in the 1991 finale, the Malaysian Grand Prix, when he came ninth, earning seven points. He rode in 41 GPs, 1992–96, without a single top-15 finish.

❀ FAST TALK (15) ❀

"Now I am five-times world champion, it is easy to say but hard to do. I am very proud. This is a world title for Spain!"
Jorge Lorenzo in November 2015

❁ LONG WAIT FOR JAPAN ❁

Japanese motorcycles have been scoring World Championship points since the late 1950s. However, Japanese fans had to wait until 1987 to attend the first 500cc Japanese Grand Prix and there were no World Championship races, 50cc to 350cc, at all between 1968 and 1987.

❁ KORK'S OFF THE PEG BIKE ❁

Kork Ballington, born in Rhodesia but representing South Africa, was a four-time Motorcycle World Champion, winning the 250cc and 350cc double in both 1978 and 1979, each time riding for Kawasaki. He had entered the World Championship in 1976 and, in his first two years, rode a motorcycle he had bought in a shop, but it was still good enough to carry him to two 350cc and one 250cc Grand Prix victories in 1977. The switch to Kawasaki took him over the top, and he was most dominant in the 1978 350cc World Championship when he won six of 11 races and took the title by 67 points. His winning margin in the 1978 250cc World Championship was a "mere" 60 points after winning seven of 12 races. Stepping up to 500cc in 1980, Ballington struggled to be competitive and finished 12th in the standings. He did, however, finish second in the 250cc World Championship, recording five victories, but he could not match four-win Anton Mang's consistency and the German took the title by 43 points. In three 500cc seasons, Ballington's best results were a pair of third-place finishes, at Assen in the Dutch TT and at Imatra in the Finnish GP.

❁ MINARELLI'S DAYS IN THE SUN ❁

Vittorio Minarelli founded his autonomous motorcycle company in Bologna in 1951. In 1967 the company became Motori Minarelli and Spain's Angel Nieto won the 250cc World Championship for the company in both 1979 and 1981 – he finished third in the 1980 standings. The company entered into a business arrangement with Yamaha in 1990 and became part of the group in 2002.

❁ IRELAND WINS IN BELGIUM ❁

New Zealand's Dennis Ireland had a short-lived 500cc Grand Prix career, making only nine starts, 1978–83 and 1986. Ireland did, however, ride a Suzuki to victory in the 1979 Belgian Grand Prix at Spa Francorchamps, and also won the 1982 Isle of Man TT Classic.

❂ VALENTINO ROSSI – THE DOCTOR ❂

Valentino Rossi, "The Doctor", one of the most charismatic racers to grace motorcycle racing, was born on 16 February 1979 in Urbino, Italy. The son of a former motorcycle racer, Graziano, Valentino's first love was karting, which he took up aged five. He won a regional championship in 1990 but could not break into the national scene.

He moved to ride bikes for Cagiva in 1993 and joined Aprilia to compete in the 1996 125cc World Championship, won his first Grand Prix at Brno, Czech Republic, and finished ninth overall. Valentino was almost unstoppable in 1997, becoming 125cc World Champion after 11 wins in 15 races. He stepped up to 250cc in 1998 and was beaten to the world title by Aprilia team-mate Loris Capirossi but, 12 months later, Valentino took the 250cc World Championship with 309 points. Honda signed him to ride for them in the 500cc World Championship. The 2000 British Grand Prix, at Donington Park, was Valentino's first victory in the premier class, but Kenny Roberts Jr dominated the 500cc World Championship. He finished runner-up to Roberts Jr but ruled the roost in 2001, winning 11 GPs out of 16 to become the last ever 500cc World Champion.

MotoGP replaced the 500cc World Championship in 2002, but no one could stop Valentino, who recorded 11 GP victories and four second places. After a third consecutive World Championship in 2003, Valentino was signed by Yamaha, but the winning didn't change. Nine victories in 2003, and 11 in 2004, meant World Championships numbers four and five for Valentino – he claimed 51 GP victories in 81 races in those five years. A sixth consecutive World Championship seemed in Valentino's grasp when he claimed pole position for the 2006 season-ending GP at Valencia. However, a crash early in the race meant he was chasing everyone and, although he finished 13th, Nicky Hayden's third place was enough to give him the title by five points.

In 2007, Valentino was relegated to third place behind World Champion Casey Stoner and runner-up Dani Pedrosa. Normal service was restored in 2008 and 2009 as he won his sixth and seventh World Championships in 500cc/MotoGP – eighth and ninth in all classes. Valentino joined Ducati in 2011, but it was a disastrous move as he managed only three podium finishes, and no wins, in two seasons. A return to Yamaha in 2013 signalled a change in fortune, though his dreams of a 10th World Championship were shattered when his penalty for a clash with rival Marc Marquez in the penultimate race meant he started the season-ender in Valencia 26th – and last – on the grid. Although Valentino passed all but three rivals, Jorge Lorenzo's race victory gave him the World Championship by five points.

Did You Know That?

Rossi was the first Italian to win the Suzuka 8 Hours Endurance race in Japan when he partnered American Colin Edwards in 2000.

● 1999 500CC FINAL STANDINGS (TOP 10) ●

Pos	Rider	Nationality	Bike	Pts
1.	Alex Criville	(SPA)	Honda	267
2.	Kenny Roberts Jr	(USA)	Suzuki	220
3.	Tadayuki Okada	(JPN)	Honda	211
4.	Max Biaggi	(ITA)	Yamaha	194
5.	Sete Gibernau	(SPA)	Honda	165
6.	Norick Abe	(JPN)	Yamaha	136
7.	Carlos Checa	(SPA)	Yamaha	125
8.	John Kocinski	(USA)	Honda	115
9.	Alex Barros	(BRA)	Honda	110
10.	Tetsuya Harada	(JPN)	Aprilia	104

● CONSTRUCTORS' FINAL STANDINGS (TOP 5) ●

Pos	Team	Nationality	Pts
1.	Honda	(JPN)	338
2.	Yamaha	(JPN)	267
3.	Suzuki	(JPN)	218
4.	Aprilia	(ITA)	93
5.	Muz	(GER)	53

● NAMES TO CONJURE WITH ●

Ago	Giacomo Agostini
The Bionic Man	Barry Sheene
The Doctor	Valentino Rossi
The Duke	Geoff Duke
Fast Freddie	Freddie Spencer
Fearless John	John Surtees
The Kentucky Kid	Nicky Hayden
Mike the Bike	Mike Hailwood
Prince of Speed	Phil Read
Roman Emperor	Max Biaggi
Spanish Smurf	Dani Pedrosa
Steady Eddie	Eddie Lawson
The Texas Tornado	Colin Edwards
The Thunder from Down Under	Mick Doohan

● 2000 500CC FINAL STANDINGS (TOP 10) ●

Pos	Rider	Nationality	Bike	Pts
1.	Kenny Roberts Jr	(USA)	Suzuki	258
2.	Valentino Rossi	(ITA)	Honda	209
3.	Max Biaggi	(ITA)	Yamaha	170
4.	Alex Barros	(BRA)	Honda	163
5.	Garry McCoy	(AUS)	Yamaha	161
6.	Carlos Checa	(SPA)	Yamaha	155
7.	Loris Capirossi	(ITA)	Honda	154
8.	Norick Abe	(JPN)	Yamaha	147
9.	Alex Criville	(SPA)	Honda	122
10.	Nobuatsu Aoki	(JPN)	Suzuki	116

● CONSTRUCTORS' FINAL STANDINGS (TOP 5) ●

Pos	Team	Nationality	Pts
1.	Yamaha	(JPN)	318
2.	Honda	(JPN)	311
3.	Suzuki	(JPN)	264
4.	Aprilia	(ITA)	94
5.	TSR-Honda	(JPN)	85

● KING OF THE MECHANICS ●

Erv Kanemoto is best known as the Honda mechanic who helped Freddie Spencer become the 500cc World Champion in 1983 and 1985 (Spencer doubled up in the 1985 250cc class – a feat that can never be repeated as 500cc was rebranded as MotoGP and 250cc became Moto2), and Eddie Lawson the 500cc World Champion in 1989. Boefore moving to Honda, he had been Barry Sheene's mechanic at Yamaha in 1981. Kanemoto later helped Luca Cadalora to win 250cc World Championships in 1991 and 1992 and Max Biaggi in 1997, all riding Hondas. He was inducted into the AMA Motorcycle Hall of Fame in 2001. Now in his 70s, the motorcycle racing fanatic is still involved as a Motorcycle Grand Prix consultant.

● ROSSI'S SUPER SEVEN HOME WINS ●

When Ducati's Casey Stoner took the chequered flag in the 2009 Italian Grand Prix at the Mugello Circuit he ended Valentino Rossi's remarkable run of seven consecutive home Grand Prix victories. Yamaha rider Rossi finished third, behind team-mate Jorge Lorenzo.

⬤ 50CC WORLD CHAMPIONS ⬤

The most junior class in the World Motorcycle Championship was for 50cc bikes. It was contested for 22 years and was succeeded by an 80cc World Championship. These men were World Champions:

50cc World Champions

Year	Champion	Country	Bike
1962	Ernst Degner	(GER)	Suzuki
1963	Hugh Anderson	(NZL)	Suzuki
1964	Hugh Anderson	(NZL)	Suzuki
1965	Ralph Bryans	(GBR)	Honda
1966	Hans-Georg Anscheidt	(GER)	Suzuki
1967	Hans-Georg Anscheidt	(GER)	Suzuki
1968	Hans-Georg Anscheidt	(GER)	Suzuki
1969	Angel Nieto	(SPA)	Derbi
1970	Angel Nieto	(SPA)	Derbi
1971	Jan De Vries	(NED)	Kreidler
1972	Angel Nieto	(SPA)	Derbi
1973	Jan De Vries	(NED)	Kreidler
1974	Hans Van Kessel	(NED)	Kreidler
1975	Angel Nieto	(SPA)	Kreidler
1976	Angel Nieto	(SPA)	Bultaco
1977	Angel Nieto	(SPA)	Bultaco
1978	Ricardo Tormo	(SPA)	Bultaco
1979	Eugenio Lazzarini	(ITA)	Kreidler
1980	Eugenio Lazzarini	(ITA)	Iprem
1981	Ricardo Tormo	(SPA)	Bultaco
1982	Stefan Dorflinger	(SWI)	Kreidler
1983	Stefan Dorflinger	(SWI)	Kreidler

80cc World Champions

Year	Champion	Country	Bike
1984	Stefan Dorflinger	(SWI)	Zundapp
1985	Stefan Dorflinger	(SWI)	Krauser
1986	Jorge Martinez	(SPA)	Derbi
1987	Jorge Martinez	(SPA)	Derbi
1988	Jorge Martinez	(SPA)	Derbi
1989	Manuel Herreros	(SPA)	Derbi

Did You Know That?

After dominating the early years of the 50cc World Championship, Japanese manufacturers concentrated on the more powerful classes.

❂ 2001 500CC FINAL STANDINGS (TOP 10) ❂

Pos	Rider	Nationality	Bike	Pts
1.	Valentino Rossi	(ITA)	Honda	325
2.	Max Biaggi	(ITA)	Yamaha	219
3.	Loris Capirossi	(ITA)	Honda	210
4.	Alex Barros	(BRA)	Honda	182
5.	Shinya Nakano	(JPN)	Yamaha	155
6.	Carlos Checa	(SPA)	Yamaha	137
=	Norifumi Abe	(JPN)	Yamaha	137
8.	Alex Criville	(SPA)	Honda	120
9.	Sete Gibernau	(SPA)	Suzuki	119
10.	Tohru Ukawa	(JPN)	Honda	107

❂ CONSTRUCTORS' FINAL STANDINGS (TOP 5) ❂

Pos	Team	Nationality	Pts
1.	Honda	(JPN)	367
2.	Yamaha	(JPN)	295
3.	Suzuki	(JPN)	153
4.	Proton KR	(MAS)	65
5.	Sabre V4	(GBR)	6

❂ PACIFIC HEIGHTS ❂

Japan's loyal and fanatical supporters had two races to follow for four years at the start of the 21st century. The Japanese Grand Prix at Suzuka was an early event – third on the calendar in 2000, and first 2001–03. Towards the end of the season, riders would return to the Land of the Rising Sun for what was called the Pacific Grand Prix. This event was held at the Motegi Circuit, which from 2004 became the host of the Japanese GP. The 500cc World Champions elect, Kenny Roberts in 2000, and Valentino Rossi in 2001, were the first two winners of the 500cc Pacific Grand Prix and the two MotoGP events went to Alex Barros in 2002 and Max Biaggi in 2003.

❂ METAL GURU AND THE LUCKY FOURS ❂

Italian legend Giacomo Agostini made the home fans at Imola happy when he won the 1972 Nations Grand Prix riding for MV Agusta. On that day, 21 May 1972, the UK Singles Chart had T. Rex at No.1 with their fourth and final No.1, "Metal Guru". Coincidentally, it was the fourth race of the season and Agostini's fourth straight win.

● ISLE OF MAN TT 500CC WINNERS 1949–76 ●

The Isle of Man TT had 250cc, 350cc and 500cc World Championship classes in all 28 years; the 125cc went from 1951–73; and the 50cc event was held between 1962 and 1968. These are the winners of the Senior TT, known as the 500cc in the World Championship:

Year	Winner	Nat	Bike
1949	Harold Daniell	(GBR)	Norton
1950	Geoff Duke	(GBR)	Norton
1951	Geoff Duke	(GBR)	Norton
1952	Reg Armstrong	(IRE)	Norton
1953	Ray Amm	(RHO)	Norton
1954	Ray Amm	(RHO)	Norton
1955	Geoff Duke	(GBR)	Gilera
1956	John Surtees	(GBR)	MV Agusta
1957	Bob McIntyre	(GBR)	Gilera
1958	John Surtees	(GBR)	MV Agusta
1959	John Surtees	(GBR)	MV Agusta
1960	John Surtees	(GBR)	MV Agusta
1961	Mike Hailwood	(GBR)	Norton
1962	Gary Hocking	(RHO)	MV Agusta
1963	Mike Hailwood	(GBR)	MV Agusta
1964	Mike Hailwood	(GBR)	MV Agusta
1965	Mike Hailwood	(GBR)	MV Agusta
1966	Mike Hailwood	(GBR)	Honda
1967	Mike Hailwood	(GBR)	Honda
1968	Giacomo Agostini	(ITA)	MV Agusta
1969	Giacomo Agostini	(ITA)	MV Agusta
1970	Giacomo Agostini	(ITA)	MV Agusta
1971	Giacomo Agostini	(ITA)	MV Agusta
1972	Giacomo Agostini	(ITA)	MV Agusta
1973	Jack Findlay	(AUS)	Suzuki
1974	Phil Carpenter	(GBR)	Yamaha
1975	Mike Grant	(GBR)	Kawasaki
1976	Tom Herron	(IRE)	Yamaha

Did You Know That?
No rider managed to win all five classes, but Mike Hailwood did win the Isle of Man TT in four classes, the 125cc (in 1961), the 250cc (1961, 1966 and 1967), 350cc (1962 and 1967) and 500cc (1961 and five in a row, 1963–67). Among 500cc winners, his 12 World Championship Manx successes are two more than Giacomo Agostini's.

❀ 2002 500CC FINAL STANDINGS (TOP 10) ❀

Pos	Rider	Nationality	Bike	Pts
1.	Valentino Rossi	(ITA)	Honda	355
2.	Max Biaggi	(ITA)	Yamaha	215
3.	Tohru Ukawa	(JPN)	Honda	209
4.	Alex Barros	(BRA)	Honda	204
5.	Carlos Checa	(SPA)	Yamaha	141
6.	Norifumi Abe	(JPN)	Yamaha	129
7.	Daijiro Kato	(JPN)	Honda	117
8.	Loris Capirossi	(ITA)	Honda	109
9.	Kenny Roberts Jr	(USA)	Suzuki	99
10.	Olivier Jacque	(FRA)	Yamaha	81

❀ CONSTRUCTORS' FINAL STANDINGS (TOP 5) ❀

Pos	Team	Nationality	Pts
1.	Honda	(JPN)	390
2.	Yamaha	(JPN)	272
3.	Suzuki	(KR)	143
4.	Proton KR	(GBR)	96
5.	Aprilia	(ITA)	33

❀ ARGENTINA'S ABSENCE ❀

The 500cc Argentina Grand Prix was off the World Championship calendar after Mike Hailwood's 1963 victory and only returned in 1982, when Kenny Roberts took the chequered flag riding a Yamaha.

❀ IT'S NOT JUST ABOUT THE MACHINE ❀

At the end of the 2003 season, Yamaha had celebrated one of their racers becoming World Champion since Wayne Rainey had clinched the 1992 crown for them. In contrast, Valentino Rossi had just secured his third consecutive MotoGP crown for Honda. Rossi, however, had announced his intention to switch to Yamaha, a move which was delayed when his employers insisted he honoured his contract until the end of 2003. Yamaha's patience paid off in 2004 when Rossi won his fourth consecutive World Championship. More importantly, Rossi emulated Eddie Lawson in 1989, by winning back-to-back 500cc/MotoGP World Championships for different marques. "Steady Eddie" won on a Yamaha in 1988 and, after switching to Honda, retained his title a year later.

● GREATEST RACES (9) – 1991 GERMAN GP ●

The 1990s produced some memorable rivalries in the 500cc World Championship. The main protagonists in 1991 were the same as in 1990, Wayne Rainey (Yamaha), Kevin Schwantz (Suzuki) and Mick Doohan (Honda), first, second and third, respectively, in the World Championship.

The trio had shared the first five rounds in 1991 as they renewed their rivalry at the long – 6.788km (4.218-mile) – notoriously fast and dangerous Hockenheimring for the German GP. Hockenheim was not a circuit for the faint-hearted and demanded respect, especially as in 1991 it seemed particularly hard on tyres.

Doohan raced into an early lead with Rainey just behind him, followed by Eddie Lawson (Cagiva) and John Kocinski (Yamaha). Kocinski crashed out on lap 9 and Doohan encountered more tyre trouble. On the 18th and final lap, Rainey led Schwantz going into the first chicane, but Schwantz used Rainey's slipstream to pass him. Rainey returned the compliment on Schwantz on the final long straight. When Rainey was braking into the next right turn, Schwantz was still on the throttle and made a spectacular pass to retain the lead. Schwantz held on to win by 0.016 seconds.

1991 German Grand Prix – Hockenheimring – Sunday 26 May

Pos	Pts	Rider (Nationality)	Bike	Time/Gap
1.	20	Kevin Schwantz (USA)	Suzuki	36m 20.491s
2.	17	Wayne Rainey (USA)	Yamaha	+0.016s
3.	15	Michael Doohan (AUS)	Honda	+8.944s
4.	13	Eddie Lawson (USA)	Cagiva	+11.568s
5.	11	Wayne Gardner (AUS)	Honda	+25.500s

Did You Know That?
Suzuki launched its RG500 with Barry Sheene in 1974, and its domination was never greater than in the 1978 500cc World Championship. All but six of the 31 points-scoring riders were on RG500s – and that half-dozen all rode Yamahas.

● MULTI-TALENTED ●

Manuel Poggiali from San Marino rode an Aprilia to win four 250cc World Championship races in 2003 and added the overall title into the bargain. Two years earlier, riding for Gilera, he became the 125cc World Champion. Poggiali was also a good enough footballer to play several games for S.S. Pennarossa, a club in Chiesanuova, San Marino.

❁ 2003 MOTOGP FINAL STANDINGS (TOP 10) ❁

Pos	Rider	Nationality	Bike	Pts
1.	Valentino Rossi	(ITA)	Honda	357
2.	Sete Gibernau	(SPA)	Honda	277
3.	Max Biaggi	(ITA)	Honda	228
4.	Loris Capirossi	(ITA)	Ducati	177
5.	Nicky Hayden	(USA)	Yamaha	130
6.	Troy Bayliss	(AUS)	Ducati	128
7.	Carlos Checa	(SPA)	Yamaha	123
=	Tohru Ukawa	(JPN)	Honda	123
9.	Alex Barros	(BRA)	Yamaha	101
=	Shinya Nakano	(JPN)	Yamaha	101

❁ CONSTRUCTORS' FINAL STANDINGS (TOP 5) ❁

Pos	Team	Nationality	Pts
1.	Honda	(JPN)	395
2.	Ducati	(ITA)	225
3.	Yamaha	(JPN)	175
4.	Aprilia	(ITA)	81
5.	Suzuki	(JPN)	43

❁ LOCAL HERO ❁

The Circuit Ricardo Tormo in Valencia is named after a local motorcycle legend, the 1978 and 1981 50cc World Champion, Ricardo Tormo. He was the first rider from Valencia to win a motorcycling World Championship. His first title came as a racer for the Bultaco factory team while, in 1981, his Bultaco was privately backed. Tormo also rolled off consecutive championships in Spain's domestic events, four in the 50cc class, from 1977 to 1980, and five in the 125cc competition, 1979 to 1983.

❁ RAIN-MASTER REIGNS ❁

The 2005 MotoGP World Championship produced a number of dramatic races including four which were rain-affected – in Portugal, China, France and Great Britain (rounds two, three, four and nine). It should be no surprise that the master of the wet was also the master of the dry, Yamaha's Valentino Rossi, who after finishing second behind Alex Barros in Portugal, won the other three, the best ride of which was in the British Grand Prix at the Donington Park Circuit.

❂ FANTASY 500CC/MOTOGP
REST OF THE WORLD STARTING GRID ❂

(to the end of the 2015 season)

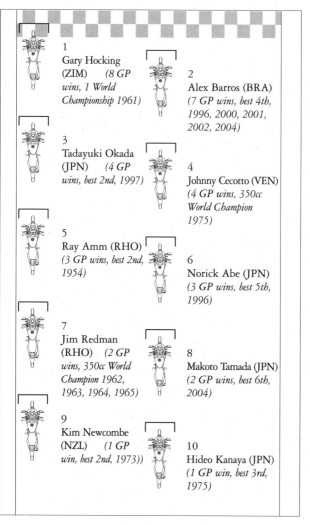

1
Gary Hocking
(ZIM) *(8 GP
wins, 1 World
Championship 1961)*

2
Alex Barros (BRA)
*(7 GP wins, best 4th,
1996, 2000, 2001,
2002, 2004)*

3
Tadayuki Okada
(JPN) *(4 GP
wins, best 2nd, 1997)*

4
Johnny Cecotto (VEN)
*(4 GP wins, 350cc
World Champion
1975)*

5
Ray Amm (RHO)
*(3 GP wins, best 2nd,
1954)*

6
Norick Abe (JPN)
*(3 GP wins, best 5th,
1996)*

7
Jim Redman
(RHO) *(2 GP
wins, 350cc World
Champion 1962,
1963, 1964, 1965)*

8
Makoto Tamada (JPN)
*(2 GP wins, best 6th,
2004)*

9
Kim Newcombe
(NZL) *(1 GP
win, best 2nd, 1973))*

10
Hideo Kanaya (JPN)
*(1 GP win, best 3rd,
1975)*

⚙ 2004 MOTOGP FINAL STANDINGS (TOP 10) ⚙

Pos	Rider	Nationality	Bike	Pts
1.	Valentino Rossi	(ITA)	Yamaha	304
2.	Sete Gibernau	(SPA)	Honda	257
3.	Max Biaggi	(ITA)	Honda	217
4.	Alex Barros	(BRA)	Honda	165
5.	Colin Edwards	(USA)	Honda	157
6.	Makoto Tamada	(JPN)	Honda	150
7.	Carlos Checa	(SPA)	Yamaha	117
=	Nicky Hayden	(USA)	Honda	117
=	Loris Capirossi	(ITA)	Ducati	117
10.	Shinya Nakano	(JPN)	Kawasaki	83

⚙ CONSTRUCTORS' FINAL STANDINGS (TOP 5) ⚙

Pos	Team	Nationality	Pts
1.	Honda	(JPN)	355
2.	Yamaha	(JPN)	328
3.	Ducati	(ITS)	169
4.	Kawasaki	(JPN)	95
5.	Suzuki	(JPN)	73

⚙ FAST TALK (16) ⚙

"The seagull wait on me for the kiss, but I told him wait on me
before the race, not the second lap."
*Andrea Iannone jokes about his collision with a seagull
during the 2015 Australian MotoGP at Phillip Island*

⚙ ONE-RACE WONDERS ⚙

The following four motorcycle manufacturers won only a single
premier-class race:

Marque	Year	Winning rider	Race
Jawa	1966	Frantisek ("Frank") Stastny	East German GP
Linto	1969	Alberto Pagani	Italian GP
Konig	1973	Kim Newcombe	Yugoslavian GP
Sanvenero	1982	Michael Frutschi	French GP

Did You Know That?
Newcombe died days after a crash at Silverstone on 11 August 1973.

● THE SUZUKI STORY ●

Michio Suzuki set up a loom works in his own name in 1909, based in Hamamatsu, Japan. They concentrated on looms until 1937, when the founder felt the company needed to diversify and they moved into cars. World War 2 put an end to the company's automotive venture, but the collapse of the silk industry in the early 1950s required another change of plan. The company returned to cars and, now, they added motorcycles to their portfolio. Their first season racing in the World Championship was in 1962, racing in the 50cc, 125cc and 250cc classes, and it was not until 1969, when a couple of riders unsuccessfully rode in the 500cc Isle of Man TT, that they entered the senior competition. The first 500cc victory came courtesy of Jack Findlay in 1971 and, five years later – courtesy of Barry Sheene – they celebrated a first 500cc World Championships, which they added to those they had claimed in the less powerful classes. That 1976 500cc season was dominated by Suzuki, with all of the 10 top finishers in the final standings riding Suzuki machines. With 90 race victories in 500cc/MotoGP, Suzuki ranks fourth on the all-time win list and their six 500cc World Championships is joint-fifth.

● BABY-FACED ASSASSIN ●

American racer Freddie Spencer (born in Shreveport, Louisiana, on 20 December 1961), was nicknamed "Fast Freddie". From the start of his full-time 500cc World Championship career – he had ridden in a single race in both 1980 and 1981 – he lived up to his nickname and on 4 July 1982, riding a Honda, he became the youngest winner of a 500cc Grand Prix, the Belgian GP at Spa-Francorchamps. He was just 20 years and 196 days old, and the following year he won the first of his two 500cc World Championships, usurping Mike Hailwood's record of being the youngest 500cc World Champion. In 1985, Freddie won two World Championships, the 250cc and 500cc titles but, in 1986 and 1987, he appeared in just six races and didn't make it to the podium. After taking a year out, Freddie returned to ride for Yamaha, but he finished 16th in the final table.

● NAZI TARGET ●

Fergus Anderson, at 44, the oldest ever winner of a 500cc Grand Prix race, in 1953, had been placed on the Nazis' "Most Wanted" list that was drawn up prior to Germany's proposed invasion of Britain.

❂ MARC MARQUEZ – THE MATADOR ❂

Marc Marquez Alenta was born on 17 February 1993 in Cervera, Spain. Few people's dreams come truer at a younger age than Marc's because his desire to be a professional motorcycle racer was achieved on 13 April 2008, aged 15 years and 56 days, when, riding for the KTM team, he made his 125cc World Championship debut in the Portuguese Grand Prix at Estoril, finishing 18th. A change to a Derbi bike in 2010 saw a change in fortune. On 6 June, at the Italian GP, Marc won his first World Championship race and he would win nine of the next 12 as he won the 125cc title, the second youngest ever, at 17 years and 263 days.

A step up to the Moto2 class in 2011 saw Marc fail to score in the first three races, but he followed that with victory in the French GP and second place at the Catalan GP. He was just three points behind German rider Stefan Bradl with two races remaining, but an injury ended his season prematurely and gave Bradl the World Championship.

Marc's decision not to move into the MotoGP World Championship paid dividends as he became the 2012 Moto2 World Champion, with nine wins in 17 races. Winning came easily to Marc, even in MotoGP, and he was on the top step of the podium, in the second race of the 2013 season, the Grand Prix of the Americas in Texas. A day after becoming the youngest ever pole-setter in 500cc/MotoGP, Marc was the youngest ever winner of a race in the class at 20 years and 63 days.

Consistency was the key to Marc's MotoGP World Championship; he was on the podium after all but two races in 2013, a retirement in Italy and a disqualification in Australia – he was one lap late in making a compulsory pit stop. His nearest rival, Jorge Lorenzo, pushed him hard, but Marc held a 13-point lead going into the final round, the Valencia GP, so if Lorenzo won – which he did – Marc needed only a top-four finish to claim the title. He took pole position, kept Lorenzo and Dani Pedrosa in sight ahead and made sure everyone else was behind. At 20 years and 266 days, Marc became the youngest ever 500cc/MotoGP World Champion.

If Marc had been good in 2013, he was almost unbeatable in 2014. In fact, for the first 10 races, he was unbeatable, setting a new record for consecutive victories in the top division. Three more wins ensured that Marc not only retained his MotoGP World Championship but also he set new records for the most wins in a season as well as the most pole positions.

Marc found things much more difficult in 2015 and his World Championship hopes were scuppered by six retirements. He still had the speed, as could be seen from those retirements, two of which came after he had set the fastest lap during the race and three when he had started from pole position. And, when things went well, wins followed, five of them in all, and this ensured that Marc finished third overall, behind World Champion Jorge Lorenzo and Valentino Rossi.

Did You Know That?
Italian legend Valentino Rossi accused Marc of helping his compatriot Jorge Lorenzo win the 2015 MotoGP World Championship by not passing him in a couple of late-season races. Adding to the intrigue, Rossi and Lorenzo ride for Yamaha; Marc is a Honda rider.

⬢ 2005 MOTOGP FINAL STANDINGS (TOP 10) ⬢

Pos	Rider	Nationality	Bike	Pts
1.	Valentino Rossi	(ITA)	Yamaha	367
2.	Marco Melandri	(ITA)	Honda	220
3.	Nicky Hayden	(USA)	Honda	206
4.	Colin Edwards	(USA)	Yamaha	179
5.	Max Biaggi	(ITA)	Honda	173
6.	Loris Capirossi	(ITA)	Ducati	157
7.	Sete Gibernau	(SPA)	Honda	150
8.	Alex Barros	(BRA)	Honda	147
9.	Carlos Checa	(SPA)	Ducati	138
10.	Shinya Nakano	(JPN)	Kawasaki	98

⬢ CONSTRUCTORS' FINAL STANDINGS (TOP 5) ⬢

Pos	Team	Nationality	Pts
1.	Yamaha	(JPN)	381
2.	Honda	(JPN)	341
3.	Ducati	(ITA)	202
4.	Kawasaki	(JPN)	126
5.	Suzuki	(JPN)	100

⬢ END OF THE ROAD FOR OPATIJA ⬢

The F.I.M. had warned the organizers of the Yugoslavia Grand Prix, at the Opatija street circuit, about its safety, with areas of solid rock walls and unprotected severe drops. They failed to improve the track's safety, with tragic consequences in 1977. Giovanni Ziggiotto was killed during practice for the 250cc race and, in the 50cc race, Ulrich Graf was fatally injured. Opatija was never used again.

❂ 2006 MOTOGP FINAL STANDINGS (TOP 10) ❂

Pos	Rider	Nationality	Bike	Pts
1.	Nicky Hayden	(USA)	Honda	252
2.	Valentino Rossi	(ITA)	Yamaha	247
3.	Loris Capirossi	(ITA)	Ducati	229
4.	Marco Melandri	(ITA)	Honda	228
5.	Dani Pedrosa	(SPA)	Honda	215
6.	Kenny Roberts Jr	(USA)	KR211V	134
7.	Colin Edwards	(USA)	Yamaha	124
8.	Casey Stoner	(AUS)	Honda	119
9.	Toni Elias	(SPA)	Honda	116
=	John Hopkins	(USA)	Suzuki	116

❂ CONSTRUCTORS' FINAL STANDINGS (TOP 5) ❂

Pos	Team	Nationality	Pts
1.	Honda	(JPN)	360
2.	Yamaha	(JPN)	289
3.	Ducati	(ITA)	248
4.	Suzuki	(JPN)	151
5.	Team Roberts	(GBR)	134

❂ THE DUCATI STORY ❂

Ducati, a family-owned business, was founded in Bologna, Italy, in 1926 by Antonio Cavalieri Ducati and his three sons, Adriano, Bruno and Marcello. Officially, the Societa Scientifica Radio Brevetti Ducati produced condensers, vacuum tubes and other radio components. In 1935, the business moved into a newly constructed factory in another part of the city. Things were very difficult in World War 2 and the company almost folded several times, especially as the factory was a regular target for Allied bombs. In 1944, Aldo Farinelli, the founder of Societa Italiana per Applicazioni Tecniche Auto-Aviatorie (SIATA), began developing a small pushrod engine, the *Cucciolo* (Italian for puppy), for bicycles in his Turin factory. More than 200,000 of these engines were sold in six years, and, in 1952, Ducati entered into an arrangement with SIATA selling bikes with *Cucciolo* engines. This first Ducati bike had a top speed of 40mph (64 kmh), and weighed 98lb (44kg).

Did You Know That?
Ducati's only Manufacturers' title was thanks to Casey Stoner in 2007.

⬢ 38 YEARS OF HURT ARE OVER ⬢

The Motorcycle World Championship, in all classes, had been British riders' domain for much of the first 30 years. However, Barry Sheene's victory in the 1977 500cc World Championship proved to be the last of the 20th century, and the barren run continued for more than a decade. Danny Kent, born in Chippenham, Wiltshire, England, on 25 November 1993, had shown flashes of potential in the first season of Moto3, riding for KTM and finishing fourth in the 2012 World Championship table. Danny took a step back in 2013, finishing 22nd in the Moto3 World Championship riding for Tech 3. There was improvement after he moved to Swedish manufacturer Husqvarna for 2014, ending up eighth in the final table.

Everything came right for Danny in 2015. Riding for Honda, the 24-year-old made a great start to the Moto3 season, winning three of the first four races. By the time the season had reached the half-way mark, he was well on his way to the World Championship, having won five times and been on the podium three more times. Sunday 30 August 2015 was a very special day for Danny as he won the Moto3 British Grand Prix at Silverstone, his first victory on home soil – indeed he had never finished better than sixth. Although the rest of the second half of the season was a little disappointing – he didn't finish better than sixth – Danny had more than enough in hand to win the World Championship, six points clear of Portuguese KTM rider Miguel Oliveira and 53 ahead of third-placed Honda team-mate Enea Bastianini of Italy. The 38-year British World Championship drought was over.

⬢ TWO-HORSE RACE ⬢

It would be a slight inaccuracy to say that Japanese manufacturers have dominated recent seasons of MotoGP, only because there are just two Japanese companies which have ruled the roost in the World Championship. You have to go back to 17 October 2010 to find the last time the top step of a MotoGP podium was not occupied by a racer who had just got off either a Yamaha or Honda motorcycle. The 2010 Australian MotoGP was won by Casey Stoner – who would begin riding for Honda the following season – riding for Ducati. Even the legendary Valentino Rossi could not win a MotoGP race when he was on a Ducati. Japan's third manufacturer, Suzuki, missed three full seasons, but had no podium finishes in 2011 or 2015. Ducati's record in that spell is at least better; they have enjoyed 14 second- or third-place finishes, and only twice have they taken both second and third spots.

● 2007 MOTOGP FINAL STANDINGS (TOP 10) ●

Pos	Rider	Nationality	Bike	Pts
1.	Casey Stoner	(AUS)	Ducati	367
2.	Dani Pedrosa	(SPA)	Honda	242
3.	Valentino Rossi	(ITA)	Yamaha	241
4.	John Hopkins	(USA)	Suzuki	189
5.	Marco Melandri	(ITA)	Honda	187
6.	Chris Vermeulen	(AUS)	Suzuki	179
7.	Loris Capirossi	(ITA)	Ducati	166
8.	Nicky Hayden	(USA)	Honda	127
9.	Colin Edwards	(USA)	Yamaha	124
10.	Alex Barros	(BRA)	Ducati	115

● CONSTRUCTORS' FINAL STANDINGS (TOP 5) ●

Pos	Team	Nationality	Pts
1.	Ducati	(ITA)	394
2.	Honda	(JPN)	313
3.	Yamaha	(JPN)	283
4.	Suzuki	(JPN)	241
5.	Kawasaki	(JPN)	144
=	Team Roberts	(GBR)	144

● MASTER RACER ●

Marc Marquez has already proved himself to be one of the finest riders in MotoGP history, and nowhere has he been more in control than in the German Grand Prix at the Sachsenring circuit. In his final season in the 125cc World Championship, 2010, he won the German GP on his way to winning the title. Twelve months later, in Moto2, he once again took the chequered flag, but no points from the first three and last two races meant he finished 24 points behind World Champion Stefan Bradl. In 2012, however, Marc won the Moto2 World Championship including, of course, victory in the German Grand Prix. The step up to MotoGP in 2013 and the fastest machines made no difference and he thus became the first rider this century to win four consecutive Grands Prix on the same circuit in three different classes. The 2013 and 2014 MotoGP World Champion, Marquez then went on to become the first racer ever to win six consecutive motorcycle racing Grands Prix at the Sachsenring. Marquez also holds the record for most consecutive MotoGP wins at two other venues: Indianapolis (five) and Circuit of the Americas (three).

❖ KING OF SPEED – HOW THINGS CHANGE ❖

The 1977 Belgian 500cc Grand Prix at the famous Spa-Francorchamps circuit witnessed what was then the highest average speed in the premier class. Barry Sheene won the race on a Suzuki at an average speed of 135.1mph (217.4km/h). Fast, no pun intended, forward to 2015 and Marc Marquez set a new speed record of 217.66mph (349.23km/h).

❖ CIRCUIT PAUL ARMAGNAC ❖

The French Grand Prix has been staged at no fewer than eight different circuits in the Motorcycling World Championship. The Circuit Paul Armagnac at Nogaro, in the south-west of the country, staged only two of them, in 1978 and 1982. The circuit is named after Paul Armagnac, from Nogaro, who was a racer in the 1950s and 1960s, who died racing sports cars in 1962.

Did You Know That?
The 1949, 1952 and 1958 French Grands Prix were not included in the World Championship. The 1949 edition was at Saint-Gaudens and it was at Pau in 1958, but neither circuit has hosted a World Championship race.

❖ SUZUKI LOOKING FOR A COMEBACK WIN ❖

Suzuki has an impressive record in the 500cc/MotoGP World Motorcycle Racing Championship with 90 victories in the premier class. Barry Sheene won two World Championships for them and four other racers have tasted success once. The team returned to the track in 2015, but has yet to yield any MotoGP victories. These are the racers who have won the most 500cc/MotoGP races for Suzuki and the years they were World Champions with the team:

Racer	Wins	World Champion
Kevin Schwantz	25	1993
Barry Sheene	18	1976, 1977
Kenny Roberts Jr	8	2000
Marco Lucchinelli	6	1981
Randy Mamola	5	
Franco Uncini	5	1982
Daryl Beattie	2	
Wil Hartog	2	

🪖 GRAND PRIX MOTORCYCLING CIRCUITS 🪖

World Championship races have been held at 70 different venues around the globe. These have included purpose-built tracks such as the Circuit de Catalunya, road tracks such as Spa-Francorchamps and city street circuits such as Montjuic. The TT Circuit Assen in the Netherlands has the distinction of being the only venue to have held a round of the World Motorcycle Championship every year since its inauguration in 1949.

Circuit	Location (Country)	Total
Assen	Assen (NED)	67
Masaryk Circuit	Brno (TCH)	45
Spa-Francorchamps	Spa (BEL)	41
Mugello Circuit	Mugello (ITA)	30
Sachsenring	Holenstein-Ernstthal (GER)	30
Jerez	Jerez de la Frontera (SPA)	29
Monza	Monza (ITA)	29
Bugatti Circuit	Le Mans (FRA)	28
Snaefell Mountain Course	Isle of Man	28
Circuit de Catalunya	Barcelona (SPA)	24
Donington Park	Castle Donington (GBR)	23
Hockenheimring	Hockenheim (GER)	23
Salzburgring	Salzburg (AUT)	22
Dundrod Circuit	Dundrod (NIR)	19
Phillip Island Grand Prix Circuit	Phillip Island (AUS)	19
Suzuka Circuit	Suzuka (JPN)	19
Imatra	Imatra (FIN)	18
Montjuic Circuit	Barcelona (SPA)	18
Jarama	Jarama (SPA)	17
Misano World Circuit	Misano Adriatico (ITA)	17
Nurburgring	Nurburg (GER)	17
Scandinavian Raceway	Anderstorp (SWE)	17
Motegi	Motegi (JPN)	16
Sepang International Circuit	Kuala Lumpur (MAL)	16
Silverstone Circuit	Silverstone (GBR)	16
Valenciana	Valencia (SPA)	16
Laguna Seca	Monterey, CA (USA)	15
Grobnik	Rijekadun, Croatia (YUG)	14
Circuit Paul Ricard	Castellet (FRA)	13
Estoril	Estoril (PORT)	13
Imola	Imola (ITA)	12
Losail International Circuit	Doha (QAT)	12

Did You Know That?

The Autodromo Santa Monica, opened in 1972, was renamed the Misano World Circuit in 2006 and then, following his death in 2011, it became the Misano World Circuit Marco Simoncelli.

● 2008 MOTOGP FINAL STANDINGS (TOP 10) ●

Pos	Rider	Nationality	Bike	Pts
1.	Valentino Rossi	(ITA)	Yamaha	373
2.	Casey Stoner	(AUS)	Ducati	280
3.	Dani Pedrosa	(SPA)	Honda	249
4.	Jorge Lorenzo	(SPA)	Yamaha	190
5.	Andrea Dovizioso	(ITA)	Honda	174
6.	Nicky Hayden	(USA)	Honda	155
7.	Colin Edwards	(USA)	Yamaha	144
8.	Chris Vermeulen	(AUS)	Suzuki	128
9.	Shinya Nakano	(JPN)	Honda	126
10.	Loris Capirossi	(ITA)	Suzuka	118

● CONSTRUCTORS' FINAL STANDINGS (TOP 5) ●

Pos	Team	Nationality	Pts
1.	Yamaha	(JPN)	402
2.	Ducati	(ITA)	321
3.	Honda	(JPN)	315
4.	Suzuki	(JPN)	181
5.	Kawasaki	(JPN)	88

● WHEN TOBACCO BACKED THE BIKERS ●

Multiple 500cc World Champion Barry Sheene was rarely photographed without a lit cigarette either between his fingers or in his mouth – and this was more than a decade after the dangers of using tobacco products were well documented. Tobacco companies began sponsoring motorcycle racing – albeit rather later than they had started pumping money into racing motorcars – but their bottomless pockets were certainly in evidence in the final table of the 1986 500cc World Championship. The top six teams were all backed by tobacco and this was how the table looked, with the sponsors' names added to the teams:

Pos	Racer	Nationality	Team	Pts
1.	Eddie Lawson	(USA)	Marlboro-Yamaha	139
2.	Wayne Gardner	(AUS)	Rothmans-Honda	117
3.	Randy Mamola	(USA)	Lucky Strike-Yamaha	105
4.	Mike Baldwin	(USA)	Lucky Strike-Yamaha	78
5.	Rob McElnea	(GBR)	Marlboro-Yamaha	60
6.	Christian Sarron	(FRA)	Gauloises-Yamaha	58

❀ NOT ALL THE GOOD TIMES ROLL ❀

The motto of Japanese manufacturer Kawasaki Heavy Industries Motorcycle & Engine is "Let the Good Times Roll". Sadly, when it came to the 500cc/MotoGP World Championship, the good times didn't really roll. The team managed just two victories in the elite class, Dave Simmonds – who had been the team's first World Champion, at 125cc in 1969 – winning the 1971 season-ending Spanish Grand Prix at Jarama. Mick Grant was also on a Kawasaki when he won the 1975 500cc Isle of Man TT – it was the penultimate year the Tourist Trophy was part of the World Championship. The real glory era for the team was between 1978 and 1982 when Anton Mang of West Germany and Rhodesia-born South African Kork Ballington both claimed a pair of 250cc and 350cc World Championships. Kawasaki returned to MotoGP in the early 2000s, but Shinya Nakano, Randy de Puniet and Marco Melandri could not finish better than tenth in the World Championship standing and the team withdrew after the 2009 season.

❀ TOP SALARIES ❀

Like almost every sport, the income of the leading competitors is boosted by huge endorsements and the actual salaries frequently are only a tiny proportion of the earnings. These were the ten highest salaries – excluding endorsements – of riders on the 2015 MotoGP grid:

Rank	Racer	Nationality	Team	Salary (US$)
1.	Valentino Rossi	(ITA)	Yamaha	$10m
2.	Marc Marquez	(ESP)	Repsol Honda	$10m
3.	Jorge Lorenzo	(ESP)	Yamaha	$6.5m
4.	Dani Pedrosa	(ESP)	Repsol Honda	$2.5m
5.	Andrea Dovizioso	(ITA)	Ducati	$1m
6.	Aleix Espargaro	(ESP)	Suzuki	$900,000
=	Alvaro Bautista	(ARG)	Aprilia Gresini	$900,000
8.	Andrea Iannone	(ITA)	Ducati	$500,000
9.	Marco Melandri	(ITA)	Aprilia Gresini	$300,000
=	Maverick Vinales	(ESP)	Suzuki	$300,000

Did You Know That?
According to the *Forbes* 2015 Rich List, retired basketball legend Michael Jordan earned around US$100 million in 2014, all from endorsements or personal appearances.

⚜ 2009 MOTOGP FINAL STANDINGS (TOP 10) ⚜

Pos	Rider	Nationality	Bike	Pts
1.	Valentino Rossi	(ITA)	Yamaha	306
2.	Jorge Lorenzo	(SPA)	Yamaha	261
3.	Dani Pedrosa	(SPA)	Honda	234
4.	Casey Stoner	(AUS)	Ducati	230
5.	Colin Edwards	(USA)	Yamaha	161
6.	Andrea Dovizioso	(ITA)	Honda	160
7.	Toni Elias	(SPA)	Honda	115
8.	Alex de Angelis	(SMR)	Honda	111
9.	Loris Capirossi	(ITA)	Suzuki	120
10.	Marco Melandri	(ITA)	Kawasaki	108

⚜ CONSTRUCTORS' FINAL STANDINGS (TOP 5) ⚜

Pos	Team	Nationality	Pts
1.	Yamaha	(JPN)	386
2.	Honda	(JPN)	297
3.	Ducati	(ITA)	272
4.	Suzuki	(JPN)	133
5.	Kawasaki	(JPN)	108

⚜ WORLD LEADER ⚜

Honda was founded in Hamamatsu, Japan, in October 1946 by Soichiro Honda, and produced piston rings for Toyota before it began selling pushbikes fitted with two-stroke 50cc generator engines. In 1949, Honda produced its first complete motorcycle and quickly acquired a good name in the industry. By 1964, Honda was the world's largest manufacturer of motorbikes – it produced three million in 1972 – as renowned for the quality of its motorcycles as it was for its range of cars and power equipment. In all, Honda has won the Manufacturers' World Championship 64 times, 21 of which have been in the 500cc/MotoGP division.

⚜ DESIGNER BROTHER ⚜

Cromie McCandless enjoyed success in the early years of the Motorcycle World Championship, winning the 125cc Isle of Man TT in 1951 and that year's 500cc Ulster Grand Prix. His brother, Rex, worked for the Norton Motorcycle Company and helped design the hugely successful "Featherbed Frame" for their motorcycles.

● GREATEST RACES (10) – 1975 DUTCH TT ●

Assen celebrated its 50th anniversary with the 1975 Dutch TT (though World War 2 caused the race's cancellation 1940–45). Barry Sheene (Suzuki) took pole, with Giacomo Agostini (Yamaha) second, followed by Teuvo Lansivuori (Yamaha), Gianfranco Bonera (MV Agusta) and Phil Read (MV Agusta).

It soon became clear that the race would be a straight battle between Sheene, in only his second season in 500cc racing, and Agostini, seven times the 500cc World Champion, and they swapped the lead lap after lap. Read, Agostini's closest challenger for the World Championship, had quickly passed the Finn Lansivuori and the Italian Bonero, and shadowed the front two from a distance.

The clock could not separate the riders as they took the chequered flag, both given 48m 1s, so a photo finish had to prove the winner. Race stewards studied the evidence and gave the race to Sheene, the first of his 19 500cc victories. This remains the closest ever finish in the history of 500cc/MotoGP racing.

Agostini won his eighth 500cc World Championship by eight points from Read.

1975 Dutch Tourist Trophy – Assen – Sunday 28 June

Pos	Pts	Rider (Nationality)	Bike	Time/Gap
1.	15	Barry Sheene (GBR)	Suzuki	48m 01.000s
2.	12	Giacomo Agostini (ITA)	Yamaha	same time
3.	10	Phil Read (GBR)	MV Augusta	+48.700s
4.	8	John Newbold (GBR)	Suzuki	+1 lap
5.	6	Tevo Lansivuori (FIN)	Suzuki	+1 lap

Did You Know That?

In 1924, the Dutch Government passed a law permitting racing to take place on public roads. The following year, the Dutch Tourist Trophy race was born.

● A GHOULISH REMINDER ●

The death of Marco Simoncelli in the 2011 Malaysian Grand Prix brought back memories of a similar incident a year earlier. On the 12th lap of the 2010 San Marino Moto2, at Misano, Japan's Shoya Tomizawa was in fourth place when he was forced wide and came off his Honda bike at the Curvone corner. Immediately behind him were England's Scott Redding and Alex de Angelis, from San Marino, and they both ran over Tomizawa, causing fatal injuries.

❀ JORGE LORENZO – YOUNG AND FAST ❀

Jorge Lorenzo was born in Palma, Majorca, Spain, on 4 May 1987. On 4 May 2002, his 15th birthday, he was a Motorcycle World Championship racer, riding a Derbi in his home 125cc Grand Prix at Jerez. There was no storybook ending but he did finish in 22nd place. No one could question Jorge's ability and he completed 11 of the final 13 races that season, collecting points four times – his best was seventh in the Brazilian Grand Prix. The season ended with Jorge on 21 points and 21st in the 125cc World Championship table.

There was something about the Autodromo Internacional Nelson Piquet, home of the Rio de Janeiro Grand Prix, that agreed with Jorge because, on 22 September 2002, he won the 125cc Brazilian Grand Prix. He finished 12th in that year's World Championship and fourth a year later. This signalled a step up the ladder, to 250cc, where he rode for Honda in 2005. A move to Aprilia the following year brought World Championship glory with 250cc titles. Jorge accepted the challenge of competing in MotoGP and was signed by Yamaha. In just his third race, the Portuguese Grand Prix at Estoril, he became MotoGP winner. It would be Jorge's only victory that season, but there were four in 2009 as he chased Valentino Rossi for the title. Eventually he finished 35 points behind the Italian, but 27 clear of everyone else. Glory, it seemed, was around the corner.

And it was. In the first 10 races, Jorge was on the top step of the podium seven times and the one below after the other three. His worst finish in 18 races was fourth place, which happened in the Aragon and Japanese Grands Prix, but he finished the campaign in style by winning the season-ending races in Portugal and Valencia. With 383 points, he had metaphorically lapped the field – Dani Pedrosa was second in the standings with 245 points. He couldn't repeat that achievement, but still finished second in the standings behind Casey Stoner. Jorge's second World Championship came in 2012 when his consistency was again the key. There were only three finishes on his record, first (six times) second (10 times) and retired (twice). Pedrosa was again his closest challenger, but he was 18 points adrift.

No one knew it at the time, but Jorge's total of 80 points in rounds 4–9 cost him the 2013 World Championship. He lost 22 points compared to Marc Marquez, and the title ended up with his young compatriot by just four points. The following year Marquez won all of the first 10 races, so the battle was for second place, and Jorge had to give best to Rossi, but he did finish third in the World Championship, amazingly his worst placing since his rookie season of 2008. The battle for the 2015 MotoGP World Championship was one of the most thrilling ever. Jorge made a great start, winning four of the early Grands Prix, including at Jerez and Catalunya. Rossi hit back, but Jorge remained, as always, metronomically consistent, and when the Italian was punished for an incident with Marquez in the penultimate race, the title was Jorge's to lose at Valencia. He started from pole position, knew compatriots Pedrosa and Marquez were his only real rivals in the race, and rode to victory in the race and the MotoGP World Championship.

Did You Know That?

Jorge is one of the most loyal racers in MotoGP, having switched teams in a class only once, when he left Honda for Aprilia after the 2005 season. In eight MotoGP seasons with Yamaha he has won 40 times.

❀ 2010 MOTOGP FINAL STANDINGS (TOP 10) ❀

Pos	Rider	Nationality	Bike	Pts
1.	Jorge Lorenzo	(SPA)	Yamaha	383
2.	Dani Pedrosa	(SPA)	Honda	245
3.	Valentino Rossi	(ITA)	Yamaha	233
4.	Casey Stoner	(AUS)	Ducati	225
5.	Andrea Dovizioso	(ITA)	Honda	206
6.	Ben Spies	(USA)	Yamaha	176
7.	Nicky Hayden	(USA)	Ducati	163
8.	Marco Simoncelli	(ITA)	Honda	125
9.	Randy de Puniet	(FRA)	Honda	116
10.	Marco Melandri	(ITA)	Honda	103
=	Colin Edwards	(USA)	Yamaha	103

❀ CONSTRUCTORS' FINAL STANDINGS (TOP 4) ❀

Pos	Team	Nationality	Pts
1.	Yamaha	(JPN)	404
2.	Honda	(JPN)	342
3.	Ducati	(ITA)	286
4.	Suzuki	(JPN)	108

❀ FAST TALK (17) ❀

"We decided to remember him with a song from Pink Floyd, that every time I hear I remember Marco. This was the idea. A tribute to him."
Valentino Rossi, who wore a specially designed helmet in honour of his friend Marco Simoncelli at the 2013 San Marino MotoGP

⬡ 2011 MOTOGP FINAL STANDINGS (TOP 10) ⬡

Pos	Rider	Nationality	Bike	Pts
1.	Casey Stoner	(AUS)	Honda	350
2.	Jorge Lorenzo	(SPA)	Yamaha	260
3.	Andrea Dovizioso	(ITA)	Honda	228
4.	Dani Pedrosa	(SPA)	Honda	219
5.	Ben Spies	(USA)	Yamaha	176
6.	Marco Simoncelli	(ITA)	Honda	139
=	Valentino Rossi	(ITA)	Ducati	139
8.	Nicky Hayden	(USA)	Ducati	132
9.	Colin Edwards	(USA)	Yamaha	109
10.	Hiroshi Aoyama	(JPN)	Honda	98

⬡ CONSTRUCTORS' FINAL STANDINGS (TOP 4) ⬡

Pos	Team	Nationality	Pts
1.	Honda	(ITA)	405
2.	Yamaha	(GBR)	325
3.	Ducati	(GBR)	180
4.	Suzuki	(ITA)	73

⬡ LEGENDS RETURN ⬡

The Assen Centennial Classic 1998 was a nostalgic celebration of the first five decades of Grand Prix racing, the heyday of the sport. This wonderful festival of speed saw more than forty World Champions from different decades come to the home of the Dutch Tourist Trophy (it has always been the TT and not a Grand Prix) at TT Circuit Assen, Netherlands. Apart from being an obvious autograph hunter's paradise with the likes of Giacomo Agostini, Geoff Duke, Phil Read, Jim Redman, Barry Sheene, Luigi Taveri and Carlo Ubbiali all in attendance, these great champions were once again seen riding the same machines upon which they claimed their world titles. The air was filled with the glorious iconic sounds of multi-cylinder four-strokes machines from AJS, Benelli, Gilera, Honda, Jawa and MV Agusta as well as the single-cylinder Norton and Matchless plus the big beasts of the two-strokes Kawasaki, Suzuki and Yamaha.

Did You Know That?
The only event at the same venue in every year of the 500cc/MotoGP Motorcycle World Championship is the Dutch (or Assen) TT, at Assen, the Netherlands. The most successful racer has been Valentino Rossi, with seven victories; the leading team is Honda, with 19 wins.

● CONSTRUCTORS' WINS IN 500CC/MOTOGP ●

Pos	Team	Nationality	Wins
1	Honda	(JPN)	263
2	Yamaha	(JPN)	235
3	MV Agusta	(ITA)	139
4	Suzuki	(JPN)	90
5	Gilera	(ITA)	35
6	Ducati	(ITA)	31
7	Norton	(GBR)	21
8	AJS	(GBR)	5
9	Cagiva	(ITA)	3
=	Matchless	(GBR)	3
=	Moto Guzzi	(ITA)	3
12	Kawasaki	(JPN)	2
13	Jawa	(JPN)	1
=	Koenig	(GER)	1
=	Linto	(ITA)	1
=	Sanverno	(ITA)	1

● THE ROMAN EMPEROR OF MOTORCYCLING ●

Massimiliano "Max" Biaggi was born in Rome, Italy, on 26 June 1971. Max was more interested in playing football than riding motorcycles until, for his 17th birthday, his parents bought him one, a gift that changed his life and destiny. In 1990, his second season riding in the 125cc class, he won the Italian Sport Production Championship. Max took to the world stage and showed off his talent by winning the 250cc World Championship four times 1994–97 inclusive. The first three titles were riding for Aprilia before he moved to Honda for the fourth World Championship. And the Japanese giants gave him the chance to compete on the biggest stage, the 500cc World Championship in 1998, riding for Team Kanemoto.

● MESTRE DE ESTORIL●

The Portuguese Grand Prix – on home soil at least – was a stop on the MotoGP World Championship calendar for 13 seasons, 2000–2012 inclusive. Valentino Rossi won the most 500cc/MotoGP races, five of them, and no one else won more than Jorge Lorenzo's three. Two teams dominated all classes at the Portuguese Grand Prix, Honda with 13 wins and Aprilia with 12.

⚽ 2012 MOTOGP FINAL STANDINGS (TOP 10) ⚽

Pos	Rider	Nationality	Bike	Pts
1.	Jorge Lorenzo	(SPA)	Yamaha	350
2.	Dani Pedrosa	(SPA)	Honda	332
3.	Casey Stoner	(AUS)	Honda	254
4.	Andrea Dovizioso	(ITA)	Ducati	218
5.	Alvaro Bautista	(SPA)	Honda	178
6.	Valentino Rossi	(ITA)	Ducati	163
7.	Cal Crutchlow	(GBR)	Yamaha	151
8.	Stefan Bradl	(GER)	Honda	135
9.	Nicky Hayden	(USA)	Ducati	122
10.	Ben Spies	(USA)	Yamaha	88

⚽ CONSTRUCTORS' FINAL STANDINGS (TOP 5) ⚽

Pos	Team	Nationality	Pts
1.	Honda	(JPN)	412
2.	Yamaha	(JPN)	386
3.	Ducati	(ITA)	192
4.	ART	(ITA)	100
5.	FTR	(GBR)	43

⚽ BIONIC BARRY ⚽

Dani Pedrosa is probably the modern MotoGP grid's unluckiest rider in terms of injuries with more than a dozen. Before him, there was Barry Sheene, who rode in the era when one of the most popular TV shows was *The Six Million Dollar Man*, the adventures of spaceman Steve Austin – played by Lee Majors – who was rebuilt with futuristic bionics which gave him superhuman powers. Sheene was slightly less fortunate in that his broken body was replaced with contemporary hardware. Sadly, there were an awful lot of his bones which needed surgical repair. These were Sheene's two worst crashes: trying to qualify for the non-World Championship Daytona 200 in 1975, he broke six ribs, his wrist, thigh, leg and collarbone; at the 1982 British Grand Prix it was both legs which were shattered. Incredibly, Sheene was back riding his Suzuki six weeks after the Daytona crash and in 1982, having been told he might never walk again, he was racing two months later.

Did You Know That?
The Six Million Dollar Man's run ended in 1978 – around the same time that Sheene's World Championship domination came to an end.

❀ CALIFORNIA DREAMIN' ❀

The first United States Grand Prix for 23 years took place at Laguna Seca, northern California, on 10 April 1988. The winner was also from California, albeit from the southern part of the state, Eddie Lawson. Riding a Yamaha he finished more than seven seconds ahead of the Honda ridden by Australian Wayne Gardner. The previous 500cc United States Grand Prix had been on 21 March 1965, at Daytona in Florida. In that race, Mike Hailwood brought in his MV Agusta more than one and a half minutes clear of American Buddy Parrott on a Norton.

Did You Know That?
The winner of both the 1965 and 1988 500cc United States Grands Prix went on to become that season's World Champion.

❀ NOT ACCORDING TO THE SCRIPT ❀

The opening race of the 1998 season was the Japanese Grand Prix at Suzuka. Mick Doohan, the defending 500cc World Champion (he had won four in a row), was a red-hot favourite to ride his Honda to victory. However, he was upstaged by a rookie, albeit the four-times winner of the 250cc World Championship, Italy's Max Biaggi. The Roman, making his first start in the 500cc World Championship, did not read the script as he took pole position in qualifying, recorded the fastest lap and brought home his Team Kanemoto Honda in first place. Doohan may have had a weekend to forget, qualifying fourth and retiring after 15 of the 21 laps, but did go on to win the World Championship, 52 points ahead of Biaggi.

❀ A PERFECT RECORD ❀

Edmund Czihak, born 20 June 1944, only competed in one Grand Prix and won it. On 28 April 1974, at the fearsome Nordschleife circuit of the Nurburgring, Czihak rode a Yamaha to victory – and set the fastest lap – in the 500cc German Grand Prix, his home race.

❀ NOT QUITE RULERS OF THE WORLD ❀

Ducati is the third most successful team in MotoGP since 2010. While Honda and Yamaha have won at every venue in MotoGP since 2002, victories at Estoril, Le Mans, Silverstone and Indianapolis are not on Ducati's honours board.

❂ MOTOGP VENUES 2016 ❂

As of 1 January 2016, the MotoGP World Championship calendar contained 18 races across five continents. This was the provisional schedule (the date is for the race itself):

Rd	Date	GP	Venue
1	30 March	Grand Prix of Qatar	Losail, Qatar
2	3 April	Grand Prix of Argentina	Rio Hondo
3	10 April	Grand Prix of the Americas	Austin, Texas
4	24 April	Grand Prix of Spain	Jerez
5	8 May	Grand Prix of France	Le Mans
6	22 May	Grand Prix of Italy	Mugello
7	5 June	Grand Prix of Catalunya	Catalunya
8	26 June	TT of Assen (Netherlands)	Assen
9	17 July	Grand Prix of Germany	Sachsenring
10	14 August	Grand Prix of Austria	Red Bull Ring
11	21 August	Grand Prix of Czech Republic	Brno
12	4 September	British Grand Prix	Silverstone
13	11 September	Grand Prix of San Marino/Rimini	Misano
14	25 September	Grand Prix of Aragon (Spain)	Aragon
15	16 October	Grand Prix of Japan	Motegi
16	23 October	Australian Grand Prix	Phillip Island
17	30 October	Malaysia Grand Prix	Sepang
18	13 November	Grand Prix of Valencia (Spain)	Valencia

❂ NEARLY MAN TRIUMPHS IN SUPERBIKES ❂

Max Biaggi was nothing if not consistent racing in the 500cc/MotoGP World Championship. After four World Championships in 250cc, he finished second three times, third three times, four and fifth in the eight seasons 1998–2005. Winning the World Championship again had to wait until he had dropped into Superbikes and he ran off two in three years, 2010 and 2012, before retiring.

❂ SAFETY FIRST ❂

For the first 38 years of the Motorcycle World Championship, every race would begin with the riders push-starting their machines. This was very clearly rather dangerous, especially if a rider stumbled as he set off – to say nothing of them carrying serious injuries and trying to jump on a moving motorcycle. This all changed from the 1987 season when clutch starts were introduced.

● LAST WIN FOR A SATELLITE TEAM ●

Despite starting from a lowly 11th place on the grid for the 2006 Portuguese Grand Prix at Estoril, Spain's Toni Elias majestically weaved his way through the traffic ahead of him to take the chequered flag for Gresini Honda by the slimmest of margins, 0.002 seconds from Yamaha's Valentino Rossi, who had started from pole. Elias's winning margin equalled the closest recorded finish in a premier class since the introduction of electronic timing, matching Alex Criville's defeat of Mick Doohan in a Honda one-two in the 1996 Czech Republic GP at Brno. Elias's victory in Portugal was also the last time that a satellite team – one related to a larger, better-funded team – won a MotoGP race.

Did You Know That?
Also at the 1996 Czech Republic Grand Prix, Valentino Rossi won his first World Championship race, riding an Aprilia in the 125cc race.

● CZECH MATE ●

Franta Šťastný won Czechoslovakia's motorcycle racing championship five times (at 500cc in 1956, 350cc in 1958, 1959 and 1965 and 250cc in 1960). He won his home Grand Prix on eight occasions (350cc in 1956, 1958–61 inclusive, 250cc in 1954 and 1960, and 500cc in 1962). In 1957 Šťastný made his debut in the World Championship, finishing fifth aboard a Jawa in the 250cc Dutch TT at Assen. He did not return to the World Championship until 1960, when he rode in the 350cc French and Nations Grands Prix, taking second place both times. His first win came in the 1961 350cc West Germany GP at Hockenheim and he finished the season runner-up to Gary Hocking in the 350cc World Championship. After another win, in the 1965 350cc Ulster GP, Šťastný enjoyed his biggest success on 17 July 1966, racing to victory in the 500cc East German Grand Prix at the Sachsenring – the only 500cc win for Czech manufacturer Jawa and the only time a Czech rider won a 500cc/MotoGP race.

● THE GRASS IS GREENER ... BUT NOT REAL ●

When you look at pictures of racers circling the Losail International Circuit, Losail, Qatar, appearances suggest that it is truly a green oasis in the United Arab Emirates desert. Not so fast: the grass is artificial and it was laid around the track to stop the sand from encroaching on to the tarmac.

◉ 2013 MOTOGP FINAL STANDINGS (TOP 10) ◉

Pos	Rider	Nationality	Bike	Pts
1.	Marc Marquez	(SPA)	Honda	334
2.	Jorge Lorenzo	(SPA)	Yamaha	330
3.	Dani Pedrosa	(SPA)	Honda	300
4.	Valentino Rossi	(ITA)	Yamaha	237
5.	Cal Crutchlow	(GBR)	Yamaha	188
6.	Alvaro Bautista	(SPA)	Honda	171
7.	Stefan Bradl	(GER)	Honda	156
8.	Andrea Dovizioso	(ITA)	Ducati	140
9.	Nicky Hayden	(USA)	Ducati	126
10.	Bradley Smith	(GBR)	Yamaha	116

◉ CONSTRUCTORS' FINAL STANDINGS (TOP 5) ◉

Pos	Team	Nationality	Pts
1.	Honda	(JPN)	389
2.	Yamaha	(JPN)	381
3.	Ducati	(ITA)	155
4.	ART	(ITA)	99
5.	FTR Kawasaki	(GBR)	46
=	FTR	(GBR)	46

◉ THE FIRST 500CC RACE WINNER ◉

AJS was the name used for cars and motorcycles made by A. J. Stevens & Co. Ltd. The company was founded in Wolverhampton in 1909 by four Stevens brothers, Harry, George, Jack and Joe Junior. Their father, Joe Senior, who owned a nearby screw company, had a good reputation for quality engineering and Stevens Screw Company built its first motorcycle with a Mitchel single-cylinder four-stroke engine in 1897. Joe Sr then concentrated on producing engines for other manufacturers. AJS-branded motorcycles production began in 1910 with the Model A. Its engine was a two-speed 298cc side-valve and was specifically constructed to conform to the maximum 300cc limit for Junior motorcycles in the 1911 Isle of Man TT Races. Jack entered the 1911 Isle of Man TT, and finished in 15th place. The first 500cc World Championship race was in 1949 and Leslie Graham rode an AJS E90 500cc bike to victory. Following the death of Harry "Ike" Hatch, AJS's Development Engineer, in 1954, the company withdrew from road racing. In 1966, AJS was sold to the Norton-Villiers Group but the AJS name was used until 1969.

✻ THE MORECAMBE MISSILE ✻

John "The Morecambe Missile" McGuinness is a legend in motorcycle racing, even if his name barely registers in the annals of the World Championship. The Lancashire-born racer appeared in only four races between 1997 and 2000, all in the British Grand Prix at Donington Park. In 1997, McGuinness rode in the 250cc race and finished 14th to collect two points. Over the next three years, he competed in 500cc class, finishing 12th in 1998 and 13th in 2000, – he retired after 23 laps in 1999. McGuinness, however, is the absolute king of the Isle of Man Tourist Trophy series, and he has won 23 times on the Snaefell Mountain Circuit, behind only the 26 of Joey Dunlop. In 2015, McGuinness broke the lap record in the Senior race – the one which used to double as the 500cc Motorcycle World Championship event – in a time of 17minutes, 3.567seconds, an average speed of 132.701mph (213.562km/h).

Did You Know That?
McGuinness's legend was confirmed in 2013 when he and Dave Molyneux were honoured with corners of the Isle of Man circuit named after them. McGuinness's is a left-hand bend on the way up to Barregarrow on the Snaefell Mountain Course.

✻ HONDA IS UNTOUCHABLE ✻

Honda has dominated the Motorcycling World Championship for most of the last half-century, but there is no doubt which was the Japanese team's best season. It was 1997, when Mick Doohan won his fourth consecutive 500cc World Championship. The team won every race, and its riders occupied the top five places in the final standings. Doohan didn't win every race, or even finish them all, but he did win 12, take second place twice and retired in the season-ender. At Jerez in the Spanish Grand Prix, Doohan was beaten into second place by home rider Alex Criville. Then, after reeling off 10 straight victories, the Malaysian Grand Prix was won by Tadayuki Okada. Finally, there was proof of fallibility, where Doohan wanted it least. In his home race, the Australian Grand Prix at Phillip Island, he had to retire after 16 laps, which gave Criville the chance to win his second race of the season. Okada proved to be the "closest" challenger to Doohan, but he was 143 points behind and Criville, who missed five races in mid-season, finished fourth. The record of 10 straight victories was matched by Spain's young superstar Marc Marquez, who opened the 2014 MotoGP World Championship with 10 wins.

⬤ 2014 MOTOGP FINAL STANDINGS (TOP 10) ⬤

Pos	Rider	Nationality	Bike	Pts
1.	Marc Marquez	(SPA)	Honda	362
2.	Valentino Rossi	(ITA)	Yamaha	295
3.	Jorge Lorenzo	(SPA)	Yamaha	263
4.	Dani Pedrosa	(SPA)	Honda	246
5.	Andrea Dovizioso	(ITA)	Ducati	187
6.	Pol Espargaro	(SPA)	Yamaha	136
7.	Aleix Espargaro	(SPA)	Forward Yamaha	126
8.	Bradley Smith	(GBR)	Yamaha	121
9.	Stefan Bradl	(GER)	Honda	117
10.	Andrea Iannone	(ITA)	Ducati	102

⬤ CONSTRUCTORS' FINAL STANDINGS (TOP 5) ⬤

Pos	Team	Nationality	Pts
1.	Honda	(JPN)	409
2.	Yamaha	(JPN)	354
3.	Ducati	(ITA)	211
4.	Forward Yamaha	(SUI)	138
5.	ART	(ITA)	17

⬤ COMPLETING A HALF-CENTURY ⬤

The Motorcycle World Championship completed its 50th season in 1998. Mick Doohan, Honda's Australian superstar, won his fifth consecutive 500cc World Championship season, Loris Capirossi of Italy was the 250cc World Champion for an Italian manufacturer, Aprilia, and the 125cc title was also won by Aprilia, with a Japanese rider on top of the standings, Kazuto Sakata.

⬤ NEW KIDS ON THE BLOCK ⬤

The 1996 500cc World Championship season saw a new team on the starting grid, Elf, from Annemasse in France, close to the border with Switzerland. The engines were made by Swissauto and they were V4 sidecar engines with a chassis built by Serge Rosset's ROC company. With sponsorship from Pepsi, the team-leader was a Spaniard, Juan Borja, but the second bike was shared by three riders with minimal success. Borja won points in six races, with a best finish of eighth in the British Grand Prix. His 34 points left him 14th in the final 500cc World Championship standings.

❂ CARL CAN WIN ANYWHERE, EXCEPT 500CC ❂

Carl "Foggy" Fogarty made his 500cc World Championship debut in 1990 and finished 18th in the final standings with three points-scoring finishes in four starts. His best result was when, in his final 500cc outing – the 1993 British Grand Prix – he finished fourth on a Cagiva. His true calling was the Superbikes World Championship, where he was masterful, winning four titles between 1994 and 1999. Forced to retire after a crash in 2000, Fogarty won again in Australia in 2014. This time, however, it was on the reality television series *I'm a Celebrity, Get Me Out of Here!*

❂ A NEAR-PERFECT RECORD ❂

Five weeks after the German Yamaha rider Edmund Czihak won the 500cc German Grand Prix, in what proved to be his only ever appearance in any class of the Motorcycle World Championship, Phil Carpenter won his only ever appearance in the 500cc World Championship. The race was the Isle of Man TT and a rainy early June meant that it was curtailed to five laps instead of seven. Carpenter, born 14 July 1947, was no stranger to the Sneafell Mountain Course, havine raced there on previous occasions, including two 1973 World Championship races. He had finished fifth in the 350cc and seventh in the 250cc events.

❂ WORLD CHAMP VALENTINO'S LOVE IS LOST ❂

Honda ace Valentino Rossi continued with domination of the senior class in the Motorcycle World Championship. The last winner of the 500cc title and inaugural crown-wearer of MotoGP, Rossi completed his hat-trick in 2003, with another year of motorcycle mastery. He finished on the top step of the podium nine times, took second place on five occasions and, in the other two races, he was third. When Rossi didn't win, Honda still did – on all but one occasion. Sete Gibernau of Spain managed four victories and Rossi's compatriot Max Biaggi won twice. The other race, the Catalunya Grand Prix, went to a third Italian, Loris Capirossi, on an Italian bike, a Ducati. All was not sweeetness and light, however, as Rossi refused to sign a new deal and, at the season's end, moved to Honda's biggest rivals Yamaha.

Did You Know That?
Rossi was not the only one to jump to Yamaha in 2003; he took his crew chief Jeremy Burgess with him and was World Champion again in 2004 and 2005.

❂ 2015 MOTOGP FINAL STANDINGS (TOP 10) ❂

Pos	Rider	Nationality	Bike	Pts
1.	Jorge Lorenzo	(SPA)	Yamaha	330
2.	Valentino Rossi	(ITA)	Yamaha	325
3.	Marc Marquez	(SPA)	Honda	242
4.	Dani Pedrosa	(SPA)	Honda	206
5.	Andrea Iannone	(ITA)	Ducati	188
6.	Bradley Smith	(GBR)	Yamaha	181
7.	Andrea Dovizioso	(ITA)	Ducati	162
8.	Cal Crutchlow	(GBR)	Honda	125
9.	Pol Espargaro	(SPA)	Yamaha	114
10.	Danilo Petrucci	(ITA)	Ducati	113

❂ CONSTRUCTORS' FINAL STANDINGS (TOP 5) ❂

Pos	Team	Nationality	Pts
1.	Yamaha	(JPN)	407
2.	Honda	(JPN)	355
3.	Ducati	(ITA)	256
4.	Suzuki	(JPN)	137
5.	Aprilia	(ITA)	36

❂ STONER'S 69 STEPS ❂

On 28 August 2011, Casey Stoner, racing for Honda, won the Indianapolis Grand Prix. It was his seventh Grand Prix victory of the season and he would go on to win his second MotoGP World Championship, having been Ducati's only MotoGP World Champion in 2007. This win, however, was special for Stoner because it took him to 53 podium finishes, one more than Wayne Gardner and behind only Mick Doohan, who had 95, in the record of podium finishes by Australian racers. Stoner retired after the 2012 season, with 38 wins, 11 second places and 20 third places, for a career total of 69.

❂ BLEAK DAY AT SILVERSTONE ❂

On 31 July 1983, during the 500cc British Grand Prix at Silverstone, Northern Irish rider Norman Brown Jr found his Suzuki losing power on the rain-dampened circuit. He moved to the inside lane to nurse his bike back to the pits. Sadly as he exited from Stowe, being passed by riders on his outside, Dieter Braun, also on a Suziki, ran into him. The Swiss rider was killed in the crash, as was Brown.

❂ THE CATHEDRAL ❂

The home of the Dutch race in the MotoGP World Championship is the TT Circuit at Assen, Netherlands, affectionately known to racing fans as "The Cathedral". The original Assen track was brick-paved and covered 17.75 miles (28.57km), but today the circuit is 4.545km (2.824 miles) in length and comprises 18 turns – 12 right and six left. The spectator capacity is 100,000, with 60,000 seated. The first 1925 Dutch TT (Tourist Trophy) race was staged on country roads through the villages of Borger, Schoonloo and Grolloo. Italian racer Nello Pagani won the inaugural 500cc World Championship Dutch TT on 9 July 1949 riding a Mondial. Almost 15 years later, on 27 June 1964, at the Dutch TT, Rhodesia's Jim Redman became the first racer ever to claim three Grand Prix victories on the same day, winning the 125cc, 250cc and 350cc classes – he did not compete in either the 50cc or 500cc TT races that year.

Did You Know That?
The only other man to achieve a one-day hat-trick was Mike Hailwood, who emulated Redman in 1967, not only winning the 250cc, 350cc and 500c races at the Isle of Man TT on 16 June, but also repeating the achievement a week later at the Dutch TT.

❂ THE WRONG SONG BECOMES SWANSONG ❂

On 11 July 1971, West Germany's Dieter Braun – the 1970 125cc World Champion – rode his Yamaha to victory in the 250cc East German Grand Prix at the Sachsenring. Normal protocol was followed and the national anthem of the winning rider was played. The East German Government was outraged that not only had their neighbour's anthem been played, but that the fans had joined in the singing. Their retaliation was to exclude West German racers from the following year's edition. This move only became clear to the F.I.M. shortly before the race, which went ahead with winners coming from the Netherlands, Sweden, Finland, Great Britain and Italy. The regulations having been contravened, the East German Grand Prix lost its World Championship status from 1973.

❂ AGOSTINI ENJOYS THE TASTES OF FRANCE ❂

Giacomo Agostini won the French 500cc Grand Prix four times, but he is the only man to win the race at three different venues: Le Mans in 1969 and 1970, Clermont-Ferrand in 1972 and Paul Ricard in 1975.

❂ INDEX ❂

Melandri, Marco 33, 55, 77, 87, 90, 99, 131, 132, 134, 139, 140, 143
Mendogni, Emilio 32
Metisse 19, 48
Michel, Alain 67
Middelburg, Jack 74, 75, 76, 78, 101
Milani, Alfredo 12, 16, 18, 26, 41, 52, 79
Miller, Jack 60, 87, 108
Miller, Sammy 21
Minter, Derek 28, 36, 38, 40, 46
Misano World Circuit 136, 148
Modenas 116
Molloy, Ginger 54
Molyneaux, Dave 73, 109, 151
Mondenas 114
Mondial 21, 96, 109
Moneret, Pierre 18, 20, 23
Monneret, Pierre 75, 79
Montjuic Circuit 41, 136
Monza 8, 136
Morbidella 74
Mortimer, Chas 26, 59
Mosport International Raceway 137
Motegi Circuit 122, 136, 148
Moto Guzzi 8, 12, 16, 18, 20, 21, 22, 26, 42, 65, 96, 109, 145
Motori Minareli 117
Motorland Aragon 137
Mugello Circuit 136, 148
Müller, Herman Paul 77
Muz 116, 119
MV Agusta 11, 12, 14, 16, 18, 20, 22, 23, 26, 28, 30, 32, 34, 35, 36, 38, 40, 42, 44, 46, 47, 48, 50, 52, 54, 56, 58, 59, 60, 62, 65, 67, 68, 96, 105, 145
Nakano, Shinya 55, 122, 126, 128, 131, 138, 139
Nash, Godfrey 52
Nelson, Billie 48, 52, 59, 62
Newbold, John 67, 68, 141
Newcombe, Kim 58, 59, 60, 102, 127, 128
Nieto, Angel 61, 70, 85, 91, 117, 121
Noll, Wilhelm 66

Norton 8, 10, 11, 12, 14, 16, 18, 19, 20, 22, 23, 26, 28, 30, 32, 35, 36, 38, 40, 42, 44, 47, 48, 50, 63, 65, 96, 105, 145
Nurburgring 17, 59, 136
Nutt, Les 66
O'Del, George 66
Offenstadt, Eric 56
Okada, Tadayuki 112, 114, 116, 119, 127, 151
Oliveira, Miguel 133
Oliver, Eric 66, 103
Opatija Circuit 131, 137
Owesle, Horst 66
Pagani, Alberto 26, 50, 54, 56, 59, 128
Pagani, Nello 8, 11, 12, 14, 40, 55, 91, 92, 95, 155
Papa, Marco 116
Parkes, Broc 87
Parlotti, Gilberto 73
Parrott, Buddy 42, 147
Parrish, Steve 71
Pasolini, Renzo 100
Paton 50, 52
Pau 135
Pedrosa, Dani 12, 20, 39, 41, 50, 53, 57, 77, 78, 84, 85, 91, 99, 101, 118, 119, 130, 132, 134, 138, 139, 140, 142, 143, 144, 146, 150, 152, 154
Perris, Frank 35
Pesonen, Martti 54
Petrucci, Danilo 154
Phasika Freeway 14, 85
Phillip Island Grand Prix Circuit 136, 148, 151
Phillis, Tom 32, 63, 65, 91
Pileri, Paolo 91
Pitt, Brad 11
Plaisir 98
Poensgen, Katya 68
Poggiali, Manuel 77, 91, 109, 125
Pons, Sito 77, 98
Proton KR 122, 124
Provini, Tarquinio 21, 77, 91
Puig, Alberto 12, 53, 108, 110
Puniet, Randy de 40, 43
Rabat, Esteve 53, 88
Rainey, Wayne 18, 24, 27, 45, 49, 61, 69, 81, 93, 94, 95, 96, 97, 98, 100, 101, 102, 106, 107, 124, 125

Raudies, Dirk 91
Ravel, Christian 54
Read, Phil 15, 17, 24, 28, 36, 38, 40, 46–7, 58, 60, 61, 62, 67, 68, 77, 83, 85, 91, 109, 113, 119, 141
Red Bull Ring 137, 148
Redman, Jim 47, 63, 64, 65, 77, 84, 85, 127, 155
Redmond, Jim 28, 32, 61
Reggiani, Loris 65, 110
Reims-Gueux 137
Remmert, Karl 66
Rinne, Taru 68
Robb, Tommy 54, 56
Roberts, Kenny 13, 24, 25, 30, 31, 45, 47, 61, 70, 72, 74, 76, 78, 80, 82–3, 93, 94, 101, 103, 111, 115, 122, 124
Roberts Jr., Kenny 24, 69, 83, 84, 93, 118, 119, 120, 124, 132, 135
Robinson, John 66
Roche, Raymond 76, 83, 86, 88, 90
Romboni, Doriano 114
Rossell, Elena 68
Rossi, Graziano 76
Rossi, Valentino 17, 18, 20, 24, 29, 33, 38, 41, 43, 45, 49, 55, 57, 59, 71, 72, 77, 78, 80, 81, 84, 85, 90, 91, 98, 99, 101, 107, 108, 110, 114, 115, 118-19, 120, 122, 124, 126, 128, 131, 132, 133, 134, 138, 139, 140, 142, 143, 144, 145, 146, 149, 150, 152, 153, 154
Rouen-Les-Essarts 79, 137
Rougerie, Michel 72
Ruffo, Bruno 40, 77, 91
Ruggia, Jean-Philippe 98, 100
Russell, Scott 112
Rutterford, Peter 66
Ryo, Akira 107
Saarinen, Jarno 60, 61, 70, 75, 77, 82
Sachsenring 134, 136, 148
Sabre V4 122
Saint-Gaudens 135
Sakata, Kazuto 91, 152
Salatino, Juan Carlos 35, 36, 115
Salt, Charlie 105